The Jealousy Workbook

Exercises and Insights for Managing Open Relationships

Kathy Labriola

greenery press

Published in the United States by Greenery Press. Distributed by SCB Distributors, Gardena, CA.

Contents

This book is dedicated to my best friend Renee, for being the greatest friend anyone could ask for, and being there for me through all of life's highest and lowest moments.

Introduction:

Use this book to manage your jealousy!

I am a counselor, nurse, and hypnotist in private practice in Berkeley, California, and I work with many people who are struggling with jealousy. Many of my clients are involved in some type of open relationship, either by choice or by chance. In open relationships, each partner is allowed to pursue sexual or romantic relationships with other partners outside the relationship, within the parameters of a negotiated agreement.

In my experience with clients, jealousy seems inevitable in this type of relationship. Each partner is agreeing to the unpredictability, stress, time pressures, complications, and insecurities of adding outside relationships to an existing relationship. Allowing your partner and yourself the freedom to pursue other sexual relationships is one of the hardest things you are likely to attempt in your lifetime. As a result, the experience of jealousy should not seem surprising, but rather to be expected.

I have developed many techniques and exercises to help people understand their jealousy and make it much more manageable. A few of these techniques appeared in my previous book, *Love in Abundance: A*

Counselor's Advice on Open Relationships, published by Greenery Press in 2010.

Because jealousy is the most common problem my clients experience in open relationships, many have asked me for more resources on this topic, especially a jealousy workbook to make it easier for them to confront and tame the green-eyed monster. I hope the exercises in this workbook will help to meet that need. I intend to provide immediately accessible, simple techniques that are easy to implement in the event of an intense jealousy crisis. My experience is that these exercises are even more useful if undertaken over a period of time before a jealousy crisis happens, to be more prepared and skilled in managing jealousy when it does occur.

And if you are one of those extremely rare individuals who does not experience jealousy, you may find this book useful in understanding your partners' jealousy. I have included a few simple exercises that you can put into practice when a partner is experiencing jealousy and needs your active listening, emotional support, validation of their feelings, and/or problem-solving help.

I have also worked with many clients who are in monogamous relationships, but who experience jealousy even with a monogamous partner. Some of these exercises have proven useful to them as well in identifying what triggers their jealousy, what feelings, thoughts, and physical sensations they experience during a jealousy episode, what the root causes are, and how to reduce their jealousy.

The workbook is divided into two sections. The first section is intended to give you a broader overview of jealousy: how it works and why it is so powerful. This section includes exercises which can be practiced anytime, ideally before a jealousy situation arises. This is a little bit like working out at the gym to build up your strength and stamina before running a marathon or climbing a mountain. Exercising your "jealousy management muscles" by reading and trying out these exercises is intended to make you feel calmer and more in control when you *do* experience jealousy – because you will understand your jealousy, be alert for jealousy triggers, and have some practical techniques to implement immediately when the jealousy starts.

The second section is focused on techniques to implement in a jealousy crisis. You may notice that some of these, especially in the earlier parts of the section, seem almost too simple. These techniques started out as much more complicated and, I proudly thought, sophisticated. However, I discovered that when someone is in the grip of intense jealousy, they are not usually thinking rationally, nor are they capable of implementing any complex formulas. They need something fast and simple that can be used when they are not at their best.

You are likely to find some of these exercises much more useful than others, as each person has their own unique "jealousy profile" and their own distinct needs. I would encourage you to browse through the workbook and choose a few techniques to try right away, depending on your specific concerns.

In addition to utilizing this book, I would also encourage you to seek out and use other valuable resources in managing jealousy. Many people have studied this subject and developed extremely useful resources. I have included an appendix at the end of the book that lists other books, classes, and websites, as well as podcasts and resource lists that you are likely to find helpful.

PART ONE

Understanding Your Jealousy

Chapter One:

Is an open relationship right for you?

Managing your jealousy takes a lot of hard work, and can be stressful and painful. Before you decide whether you want to take on this challenge, it is important to assess whether you are a good candidate for some type of open relationship.

Most people have gone through life assuming that they are monogamous by nature. This is partially because they have been influenced by the models they see around them in a society that only values monogamous relationships, and by cultural and religious values instilled in childhood. Until they get involved with a partner who wants an open relationship, or are otherwise exposed to new models of relationships, they have no context to understand alternatives to monogamy. However, many people try to be polyamorous, due to pressure from a partner or their peer group, without carefully assessing whether this relationship style is right for them.

This assessment is a crucial step in deciding whether to pursue an open relationship and work through your jealousy. If in fact you have an inherent inclination towards monogamy, a non-monogamous relationship may not be feasible for you, and it may not be fruitful to struggle with your jealousy. Utilize the following two exercises to assess the authentic relationship orientation that best meets your needs.

Exercise One. Your relationship role models

This exercise is designed to help you see how you may have been influenced by relationships you have observed, as well as your own relationships.

Step One: What role models have you had for relationships?

Think about the relationships you have seen throughout your life, starting with the family in which you were raised.

In your childhood home, was there a monogamous relationship? This question may be difficult to assess, as you may not know whether your parents were monogamous or whether one or both had affairs or outside relationships. If you believe that their relationship was monogamous, did it seem like a healthy and happy relationship to you? Did your parents stay together as a couple throughout your childhood, or did they separate or divorce? Did either parent develop a new relationship or remarry, and did you have any stepparents? What about other relatives, such as aunts, uncles, and grandparents? Did they appear to be in monogamous relationships or not? Were these healthy relationship models for you?

During your childhood, did you see examples of "cheating" or affairs, and if so, what were the consequences of those relationships? What about other adults in your life during your childhood, such as teachers, mentors, friends of the family, parents of your schoolmates: were they in monogamous relationships or some other form of relationship? Did those relationships seem stable and successful? Did you see any examples of open relationships among any of the adults during your childhood? If so, did they seem healthy and harmonious to you? Looking at all these relationships, write down below the ones that seemed happiest or that you may have wished to emulate, such as "my mother and stepfather," or "my best friend's parents," or "my uncle and his boyfriend."

The healthiest relationships I have seen:

a._____

b._____

c._____

d._____

Step Two: Key qualities of the happiest relationships you have observed

Now, looking at those relationships that seemed healthy to you, write down the key components that you observed in those relationships which made them successful and satisfying. These may be qualities such as:

"My mom always praised my dad and listened supportively to him talking about his work," or

"My father was always affectionate to my mom and treated her with respect," or

"My aunt and uncle always seemed like a great team, always talking through things to make collaborative decisions," or

"Both of my moms had independent lives and careers; they gave each other a lot of freedom and autonomy, but loved each other deeply and were very close emotionally."

"My friend's mother had a great boyfriend who lived with them. They always seemed to really be fond of each other and have a great time together, talking and laughing together all the time."

a._____

b._____

c._____

d._____

Step Three: What healthy relationships have you seen as an adult?

Now think about all the relationships you have seen in your adult life, your own past relationships and those of friends, siblings, colleagues, and other people you have known. First, list the names of people you know in any healthy and successful monogamous relationships that you have seen. Then list the names of people in any healthy open relationships you have observed or participated in. You may not be sure whether these relationships were monogamous in practice, as some people nonconsensually have affairs and some people may keep the non-monogamous nature of their relationships private. In some cases, you will have to make your best guess about whether the relationship is monogamous or not.

Healthy monogamous relationships:

a._____

b._____

c._____

d._____

Healthy open relationships:

a._____

b._____

c._____

d._____

Step Four: List the most important components that make these relationships healthy

As in Step Two, above, list the qualities of these relationships that you believe makes them happy and successful.

a._____

b._____

c._____

d._____

This exercise is intended to give you a clearer idea of what components make a relationship successful. The next step is to identify what type of relationship is likely to work best for you.

Exercise Two: Clarify your relationship orientation

This exercise will help you assess whether you are likely to be satisfied with a monogamous relationship or not. Are you polyamorous or monogamous by orientation, or somewhere in between?

Step One: What is your experience in a monogamous relationship?

Think about each of the monogamous romantic relationships, if any, you have been involved in throughout your life. Answer the following questions:

- Did you feel safe and secure due to sexual exclusivity in this relationship? ☐ yes ☐ no

- Did you experience deeper intimacy? ☐ yes ☐ no

- Did you feel more comfortable in this relationship? ☐ yes ☐ no

- Were you able to be very honest with your partner about your feelings and needs? ☐ yes ☐ no

- Did you feel sexually satisfied in that relationship? ☐ yes ☐ no

- Do you believe that your partner was honest with you about their feelings and needs? ☐ yes ☐ no

- Did you find yourself being more focused and productive in your work and other life activities during this relationship? ☐ yes ☐ no

- Did you feel that you and your partner were a good team and became more effective and creative through the synergy of this relationship than either of you had been on your own? ☐ yes ☐ no

- Did you enjoy spending most or all of your free time with your partner during that relationship, and spending very little time alone or with other friends? ☐ yes ☐ no

Give yourself 10 points for each "yes" answer. If you scored more than 40 points, you may be more naturally inclined towards a monogamous relationship than an open relationship.

However, answering the following questions will help you make a more complete assessment:

- Did you struggle with sexual and romantic desires towards other people while in this relationship? ☐ yes ☐ no

- Did you feel bored with your sexual relationship? ☐ yes ☐ no

- Did you want more romance and excitement in your relationship? ☐ yes ☐ no

- Did you long for more emotional intimacy than your partner could provide? ☐ yes ☐ no

- Did either you or your partner "cheat" and have sex with someone else During the course of this relationship? ☐ yes ☐ no

- Did you ever feel suffocated and try to create more distance, saying things like "I need more space," "I need some time alone," "I feel too controlled," or "I want more privacy"? ☐ yes ☐ no

- Did you sometimes feel there was some important component missing from the relationship? ☐ yes ☐ no

- Did this relationship end because you lost interest in your partner after a short time and wanted to pursue a new relationship with someone else? ☐ yes ☐ no

Give yourself 10 points for each "Yes" answer in this section. If you scored more than 40 points, you may be more oriented towards an open relationship.

Step Two: Where do you fall on the relationship orientation scale?

What if you scored high on both tests?

If you scored above a 40 on both of the tests in Step One, you may be somewhere in the middle on the monogamy/polyamory spectrum. Usually, this means that there are some things about a monogamous relationship that really work for you, but some things about an open relationship that are very appealing to you. This indicates that you may be happiest in a monogamous relationship with the right person, the right circumstances, and during a particular period of your life. However, you may be just as happy in an open relationship, depending on the partner or partners, your life situation, and the specific developmental stage of your life.

Kinsey Scale of Sexual Orientation

Heterosexual			Bisexual			Gay/Lesbian	
0	1	2	3	4	5	6

Relationship Orientation Scale

Monogamous		Can be monogamous or open			Polyamorous	
0	1	2	3	4	5	6

Some people believe that polyamory and monogamy can accurately be described as relationship orientations, similar to the sexual orientations of straight and gay. This is a theory rather than a scientific fact, and more research may clarify whether relationship orientation can be as fixed as being straight or gay. The Kinsey Scale for sexual orientation places heterosexuals at zero on the scale, with gay men and lesbians at six on the scale. However, many people are bisexual and may have relationships with people of all genders, and they can be anywhere from one to five on the Kinsey Scale. Similarly, many people can be attracted to both monogamy and polyamory, and may be capable of succeeding in both types of relationships. Sexual orientation can be situational for some bisexuals, and relationship orientation may be situational for may people on the mono/poly scale as well. While the truly monogamous people may be at zero on the scale and the truly polyamorous people at six, many others may be between one and five on the relationship orientation scale. To assess where you fall on this scale, ask yourself the following questions:

- Have you found it difficult to remain sexually exclusive with a partner for two years or more? ☐ yes ☐ no

- Have you practiced what is sometimes called "serial monogamy": being exclusive with one person for a period of time but ending each relationship in order to pursue someone new? ☐ yes ☐ no

- Do you enjoy the security and stability of a monogamous relationship but also long for more romance and passion? ☐ yes ☐ no

- Have you often found yourself in a relationship where one partner has a much greater desire for sex than the other? ☐ yes ☐ no

- Have you had one relationship after another where some components of the relationship are extremely satisfying but you experience a scarcity in other areas of the relationship, such as not enough time, not enough intimacy, not enough common interests, etc.? ☐ yes ☐ no

If you answered "yes" to most of these questions, you probably have what I call a "mixed relationship orientation." This means you are likely to be able to be happy in either a monogamous relationship or an open relationship, depending on the specific situation.

Step Three: Examine your experience in open relationships

If you have already had some relationships which were consensually non-monogamous, looking a little closer at that experience can help you further assess your relationship orientation. Think carefully about the specifics of an open relationship you have been in previously or your current relationship if it is open. Answer the following questions:

- Have you felt a sense of freedom in this relationship that has been absent in previous monogamous relationships? ☐ yes ☐ no

- Does it somehow "just feel natural" to you to pursue friendships and romantic relationships concurrently with more than one person? ☐ yes ☐ no

- Have you generally made good choices in picking emotionally healthy partners? ☐ yes ☐ no

- Do you feel able to manage your time and energy in meeting the needs of more than one relationship? ☐ yes ☐ no

- Are you able to be honest with your partners about other relationships and meet their needs for disclosure of important information? ☐ yes ☐ no

- Have you generally succeeded in keeping agreements you have made with your partners? ☐ yes ☐ no

- Do you experience a spiritual component of having multiple relationships, and do you feel enriched spiritually by practicing polyamory? ☐ yes ☐ no

- Have other people mentioned that you seem to thrive and be happier when you are in an open relationship? ☐ yes ☐ no

Give yourself 10 points for each "Yes" answer. If you scored over 50 points, you are probably oriented towards having open relationships, and you have a reasonably good skill set to succeed in such relationships.

If you have determined that your relationship orientation is monogamous, then you are unlikely to be happy in an open relationship, and you would be wise to avoid anything outside of a sexually exclusive relationship. This may seem like a ridiculously obvious "no-brainer." However, in my counseling practice, I see people every day who have ignored this basic advice and entered into an open relationship even though they know that their orientation is firmly in the monogamous camp.

Sometimes this happens because they have become hopelessly attracted to or even fallen in love with someone who is polyamorous, and they could not resist the intense draw towards that alluring person despite their best intentions. They often say things like "He is the perfect man for me, except that he won't be monogamous," or "We're completely compatible in every way, except she's poly," "We are just meant for each other, we're soul mates, but he's married to someone else and won't leave her." Someone in the throes of this type of passionate love may not hear the irony in these statements, which are a lot like saying "We're perfect for each other except that we are completely incompatible." They are so intent on making it work against all odds that they cannot see that the relationship is doomed to failure by this most basic difference. They may spend years trying to change themselves to be able to accept polyamory or demanding that their partner change to become monogamous. Only after long periods of intense suffering and turmoil do they grasp that polyamory and monogamy are mutually exclusive.

Other times this mistake occurs accidentally, because one person doesn't realize that they are oriented towards monogamy, or the other person has not yet realized that they are polyamorous by nature. When their relationship orientations and world views collide, they may spend years creating pain for each other before one or both people realize that they are hopelessly incompatible because one partner needs an exclusive relationship and the other needs an open relationship.

In the worst cases, one person is well aware of their orientation but deliberately deceives the other about it until the partner is already hopelessly invested in the relationship. One partner may lie about their need for monogamy because they are so attracted to this partner that they hope one of them can change. Or the polyamorous partner may hide their orientation because they hope their partner will be able to adapt to it once the relationship is firmly established. When the deceived partner discovers the truth, they are so engaged in the relationship by then that it is very difficult to leave. And trust is destroyed by this dishonesty, adding to the feelings of betrayal.

The wisest advice is to avoid getting romantically involved with someone who doe not share your relationship orientation. However, even with the best of intentions, we can find ourselves falling for someone who will not be compatible. Once smitten, we usually put each other through hell before someone has the good sense to end the relationship and seek a partner who is more compatible.

Chapter Two:

Identifying and grieving your losses in an open relationship

When a couple decides to open their relationship, they are usually focused on what they hope to gain through having other partners. They usually expect that this change will enrich both of their lives individually through increased emotional intimacy, sexual variety or more frequent sex, and the excitement of romantic attention from someone new. Most couples also hope to experience enhanced emotional and sexual intimacy in their primary relationship. This enhancement is often fostered by the greater level of honesty and communication required for an open relationship, as well as the paradoxical experience of appreciating their relationship more because someone else is pursuing their partner. A couple can no longer take their relationship for granted when each spouse is involved with other partners, and suddenly a spouse can seem more attractive and valuable when other people are asking them for dates.

So there are many wonderful gains to enjoy, but it is important to recognize that you will also experience losses if you open your relationship. In the excitement of being "a kid in a candy store" and seeing all the possibilities for personal growth and an abundance of

love, many people fail to notice what they are losing. It is important to make a "cost-benefit" analysis so you can make a conscious choice, weighing what you hope to receive through becoming polyamorous against what you will be giving up. Most people find that all the gains in the "pros" column outweigh the losses in the "cons" side, convincing them that having an open relationship will make them happier than continuing in a monogamous relationship. The exercise in this chapter will allow you to do your own cost-benefit analysis to make sure you will not be giving up something that is precious to you, thus undermining your relationship and your quality of life.

If you decide to proceed with an open relationship, it is important to acknowledge and grieve the losses you are voluntarily accepting. There is a cost to any major change in your relationship, just as in any big decision you make in other arenas of life. For instance, if you decide to change jobs after investing many years with one employer, you are giving up job security, accrued benefits, and good wages. You may make that decision because those losses are acceptable, the new career you are pursuing is more satisfying, and in the long run you will achieve more financially and professionally. But you would not make that change without carefully looking at what you are giving up and how that compares with what you will gain. And you are taking a leap of faith into uncharted territory, which is frightening and disorienting. Similarly, with an open relationship, you must decide what losses are acceptable and whether the risk is worth taking, in comparison with the positive outcomes you are likely to experience.

Exercise Three: Your cost-benefit analysis

What will you lose by opening your relationship? For most people, sexual and romantic exclusivity are both extremely precious, and their value may not be completely apparent until they are surrendered. Think about what aspects of a monogamous relationship have been most valuable to you, and what these mean to you. It can be helpful to consider how you will feel about relinquishing these aspects of your relationship.

Step One: Evaluate the costs and benefits

Look at the two lists below, and circle the ones that are most valuable to you. These lists are not comprehensive, as they are compiled from statements made by my clients about what they have experienced and what they value most. Feel free to add anything else you have experienced, which may not be included. If you are already engaged in an open relationship, this exercise can still be helpful in identifying what you are giving up.

Benefits of a monogamous relationship

- feeling secure in my relationship

- feeling special and unique as "the one and only" partner

- believing my partner is attracted only to me

- knowing my partner will always prioritize me

- having my partner's abiding loyalty and commitment

- spending most of our free time together

- feeling protected from sexually transmitted infections

- the stability of being able to plan our future together

- feeling safe to open to a deep level of intimacy with my partner

Costs of a monogamous relationship

- feeling controlled or restricted

- sometimes experiencing boredom

- sexual problems: not enough sex, differences in sexual needs, loss of passion

- falling into patterns which make can growth and change difficult

- experiencing scarcity: of emotional intimacy, of time, of intellectual connection, of affection, of sex, or of romance

Benefits of an open relationship

- more sex
- more sexual variety
- feeling more free
- more privacy in my personal life
- more romantic attention
- feeling more sexually attractive and desired
- personal growth and learning new skills
- bringing out different aspects of myself
- more emotional support
- more practical support when needed
- feeling less dependent on my partner
- being more honest with my partner
- opportunities for more emotional intimacy
- having more choices in life
- feeling more alive
- greater confidence and self-esteem
- feeling of more abundance and less scarcity
- feeling more satisfied with my primary partner

Costs of an open relationship

- not being sure what I can count on
- being demoted from being "the one and only"
- having to negotiate over scheduling
- less time and attention from my partner
- feeling our love is "cheapened" or diluted by having other relationships
- potential risk of sexually transmitted infections
- not having guaranteed access to my partner
- fearing that other partners may replace me

- knowing my partner is attracted to others
- sharing my partner's attention and loyalty with others
- having relationship agreements that can change
- feeling less secure about the future of my relationship
- lots of "surprises" that can disrupt my life
- too much processing about jealousy and other problems

You may notice that the lists of both benefits and costs of a monogamous relationship are shorter than those for an open relationship. This does not indicate that one type is superior, it only means that most people see monogamous relationships as much simpler and easier, while open relationships involve many more variables and complications.

Step Two: Assess the value of each cost and benefit

Next, copy over each of the costs and benefits you circled in the space below. Next to each one, write down how valuable that is to you, on a scale of one to ten, in order to recognize how important it would be to you to have that benefit or how costly it would be to lose it.

Most important benefits of monogamous relationship   Value or importance

_____

_____

Most important costs of monogamous relationship   Value or importance

_____

_____

Most important benefits of an open relationship   Value or importance

_____

_____

Most important costs of an open relationship   Value or importance

_____

_____

An example:

Sandy wrote down that she had circled these benefits and costs of monogamy as being the most important to her:

Benefits of monogamous relationship	Value or Importance
feeling special and unique as "the one and only" partner	10
believing my partner is attracted only to me	8
feeling safe to open to a deep level of intimacy with my partner	10

Costs of monogamous relationship	Value or Importance
falling into patterns which make can growth and change difficult	8
experiencing scarcity: of affection and of romance	8

She then wrote that she had circled these benefits and costs for an open relationships:

Benefits of an open relationship	Value or importance
feeling of more abundance and less scarcity	10
feeling more satisfied with my primary partner	7
more romantic attention	8

Costs of an open relationship	Value or importance
not being sure what I can count on	8
being demoted from being "the one and only"	10
feeling our love is "cheapened" or diluted by having other relationships	8
knowing my partner is attracted to others	9

From doing this exercise, Sandy realized that if she and her husband pursued an open relationship, the two greatest "costs" to her would be giving up feeling special and unique as the one and only partner, and giving up her belief that her husband was not attracted to anyone else except her. In thinking about this, she had to admit that she had always known that her husband had been attracted to other women, but she had created a comforting fantasy that he only had eyes for her. Giving up that belief would be painful but was a recognition of reality rather than any real change, and that realization made it easier. In looking at the cost of feeling less special if her husband slept with other women, she realized that it would be extremely painful to accept being "demoted from being the one and only." She knew that this would trigger intense jealousy for her, and that this would be the focus of her work with her counselor to learn to feel secure, special, and deeply loved even if she was no longer the only lover.

She also was surprised to see that staying in a monogamous relationship also had costs for her: that she and her husband had fallen into some frustrating patterns in their relationship which made her feel stuck and had stymied her personal growth. In addition, she experienced chronic scarcity of affection and romance, in that her husband had never been that big on making romantic gestures like love notes or telling her he loved her, and she was excited about having outside partners who might provide additional affection and romance so she would feel more satisfied in her primary relationship.

In looking at the overall cost-benefit analysis, Sandy decided that she was willing to give up sexual and romantic exclusivity with her husband and have an open relationship. She experienced some grieving over the losses this entailed, especially fears of her love being "cheapened" and not feeling unique. However, she described polyamory as "a net gain," because as she predicted, dating other men increased her overall satisfaction by giving her lots of affection and romance, and as an added bonus her husband became much more affectionate and attentive when so many other men were expressing interest in her.

Chapter Three:

Understanding your jealousy

What is jealousy? Jealousy is a complex combination of feelings, sensations, experiences, and reactions triggered by a fear of loss or change in a valuable relationship, job, position, resource, or status. While we tend to think of jealousy only in relation to romantic or sexual relationships, jealousy is present in our lives literally from birth. Jealousy occurs in a wide variety of situations: in our families of origin, at school as kids, in our careers, in civic and community service organizations, and even in our hobbies. Most people handle jealousy much more comfortably in situations other than love relationships. It can be very useful to look at how you respond to a jealousy-provoking situation outside your romantic relationship – for instance, sibling rivalry, or finding yourself competing with a co-worker for a promotion. It is fairly likely that in such situations, you don't become incapacitated by jealousy or act out in a way that you will later regret. Looking at how well you handle jealousy in that situation can help you realize that you are in fact capable of managing jealousy and having a different response. Often it will be possible to transfer that skill back to your romantic relationship, building confidence that your response will be more rational and constructive. Try this exercise to strengthen your ability to react to jealousy with more clarity and stability.

Exercise Four: Jealousy through the life span

Step One: Childhood experiences of jealousy

Think back on your childhood and see if you recall experiencing jealousy in any of the following situations. Underneath each one that has been true for you, write a number between 1 and 10 to rate the intensity of the jealousy you experienced. Then write down what you can remember about how you handled the situation, what you did to address it, whether you feel your response was successful in resolving your jealousy, and whether or not you're comfortable with the outcome of the situation itself.

General examples:

- Your parents were busy with their work or other activities and didn't give you as much time and attention as you wanted.

- The birth of a new sibling suddenly took all the attention away from you and focused it on the new baby.

- A parent seemed to like another sibling more, or another sibling was better behaved, did better in school, or was more successful socially.

- You didn't get picked for the football team, but your friends made the team.

- Your best friend started spending more time with another friend.

- A friend became more popular than you and was invited into a "cool" clique.

- Other friends seemed to get more dates than you did.

- A friend got better grades and got into a better college.

A personal example:

Situation: A friend becomes more popular than you and is invited into a "cool" clique.

Jealousy Intensity Level: 7

How did I handle it? "I was devastated that my friend abandoned me during our freshman year of high school when she became friends with some popular kids, and I envied her for being "in" with that crowd. At first, I sulked and was rude to her when I ran into her in the halls or in class. I was already involved in the drama club when this happened, and in order to distract myself from feeling humiliated, I tried out for and got the lead role in the school play – that significantly improved my self-esteem. I made some really great friends through being involved in the play, who were not nearly as shallow as the clique my ex-friend was involved with."

How did I feel about my response and the outcome of the jealousy situation? I totally got over my jealousy and began being friendly to her when I ran into her. We actually became good friends again in our junior and senior years. I think this was a really functional way to handle jealousy: doing something that would increase my confidence and self-esteem as well as distract me from my pain, and making some new friends so I didn't feel envious or abandoned.

Step Two: Jealousy in non-romantic relationships in adulthood

In adulthood there are also many experiences which may provoke intense jealousy, in situations that have nothing to do with romantic relationships. Read over the following list and see if you have experienced jealousy in any of these circumstances. As with Step One, think back on your adult life and see if you recall experiencing jealousy. Underneath each one that has been true for you, write a number between 1 and 10 to rate the intensity of the jealousy you experienced in each situation. Then write down what you can remember about how you handled the situation, what you did to address it, whether you feel your response was successful in resolving your jealousy, and whether or not you were comfortable with the outcome of the situation itself.

General examples:

- Your neighbor has a nicer house than you or buys a very expensive car.

- Your co-worker gets the promotion you applied for.

- Your boss refuses to give you a raise but gives another co-worker a raise.

- Your best friend marries someone with a lot of money, or who is much better-looking than your spouse.

- Your partner spends too much time at work, on sports, on the computer, or on hobbies and not enough time with you.

- Your partner would rather drink or use drugs than spend time with you.

- Your neighbor's kid gets into Harvard and your kid is unemployed and undirected.

- Your friends all have grandchildren but you have none.

- Your partner seems more loyal and committed to their children from a previous marriage than to you.

An example:

Situation: Jill's partner Mitch spent too much time at work, and often worked late and didn't get home in time for dinner, and often worked from home on the weekends.

Jealousy Intensity Level: 8

How did she handle it? Jill made a date with her partner in advance to sit down and talk about the situation. She also wrote him an email explaining that she was feeling lonely and wanted more quality time with him, especially on weekends. They had two long conversations about the situation, since during the first one she had gotten upset and started crying, and couldn't be a very good listener. The second time, she was able to just keep breathing and talk to him without being accusative and judgmental, but just kept telling him how much she loved him and how important it was to have time together on the weekends and a few evenings a week. She also made a point of repeatedly telling him how much she appreciated his dedication to his work, how hard-working and responsible he was, how his hard work had brought promotions and raises which had allowed them to have a very comfortable standard of living, and what a good provider he was for the family.

Mitch agreed not to work on Sundays at all, so they would have at least one weekend day to be together, and he agreed to be home for dinner at least one or two weeknights each week. Jill agreed not to complain or nag him and to be appreciative and validate his hard work.

How did she feel about her response and the outcome of the jealousy situation? The discussions brought them closer, and Mitch felt more appreciated and loved, and less stressed about her complaints. Jill felt more secure that they would have enough quality time together.

Step Three: Write down below the answers to the following questions:

What did you learn about your jealousy from these two exercises?

_____

_____

_____

Is there a strategy or coping mechanism you used in these situations that could be used to help you in responding to romantic jealousy the next time it occurs?

_____

_____

Use the answers to these questions to plan ways to better handle jealousy when it does occur.

Chapter Four:

What triggers your jealousy?

Now that you have been able to define the emotions you experience when you are jealous, and identified the costs and benefits of an open relationship, it's time to figure out what exactly triggers your jealousy. Every person will discover that a different constellation of situations, events, and behaviors can suddenly throw them into an intense jealousy episode. If you can predict in advance what these "triggers" are, you can find ways to avoid them or manage them.

Exercise Five: Guided imagery exercise to visualize your jealousy triggers

"Visualization" or "guided imagery" are similar to meditation. They are structured methods of relaxing as much as possible and imagining a specific scenario, in order to rehearse and master that situation. These techniques often help people get down to the "nitty gritty" of what is causing jealousy.

Step One: Get comfortable and relaxed

Set aside at least thirty minutes when you can have privacy and quiet. Get in a comfortable position, close your eyes, and take a few deep breaths to try to become more comfortable and relaxed.

Step Two: Imagine your partner in a romantic situation with someone else

Visualize your partner initiating a new relationship with someone else, either someone they are currently interested in or already involved with, or with an imaginary "hypothetical lover." Imagine this situation as clearly and vividly as possible, despite any discomfort or anxiety. Try to become aware of the sight of your partner relating to another person, the sounds of their voices, the feel of them touching, even the smell or fragrance in the environment they are in. Get as complete a picture as you can of them being in the same space together.

Step Three: Watch the entire scenario unfold

Imagine them together as if you were watching a film of the entire process. Begin with when they first meet, the initial spark of interest, being on a date, going out, having a meal together, perhaps hugging or having some non-sexual affection.

Step Four: Pause the scene whenever you feel uncomfortable

As if you had a remote control, press the pause button for a few moments at any point along the way where you feel discomfort or jealousy. Try to identify exactly what mix of emotions you are actually feeling at different points as the scenario unfolds.

Step Five: Continue to visualize them together

If you feel able to continue, visualize your partner going home with this new person, getting undressed, and having sex. Again, press the pause button for a few moments whenever you feel any painful emotions. This exercise will be the most useful if you imagine the sounds, smells, touch, and tastes of this experience. If you become too triggered, stop here and try this exercise again when you are feeling more comfortable.

Step Six: The night and the morning after

If you feel able to continue, imagine your partner being with this new person after having sex, sleeping together overnight, and waking up in the morning. Now visualize your lover coming back to you and telling you about the relationship, noticing how your lover treats you, and what it feels like for your being with your partner again after they have been with someone else.

Step Seven: Clear the screen

Take a few deep breaths, deliberately let all those images fade away, and imagine clearing the screen. Now, think of a very pleasant and happy experience you have had with your partner any time during your relationship, and visualize that scene in your mind's eye to replace any lingering images. Count to five and open your eyes.

Step Eight: Write down the triggers you experienced

Write in the space below any moments when you became jealous or uncomfortable during this visualization. Write down exactly what was happening between your partner and the other person when you were triggered. Then write what specific emotions you were feeling at that moment.

Trigger:_____

Feelings:_____

Trigger:_____

Feelings:_____

Trigger:_____

Feelings:_____

Most people are surprised to find that visualizing their partner having another relationship like this is generally painless except at certain key moments. When you discover exactly what triggers your jealousy, it puts things in perspective. Realizing that you are only jealous of one or two pieces of the overall picture makes it much more manageable.

Some examples:

Kim discovered that going through the entire sequence was actually pleasurable, except that she freaked out at visualizing Will getting into "their" bed with another woman. She made an agreement with him that he would only sleep with other women outside their home, either at the woman's house or at a hotel, so she would feel safer.

Mark was surprised that he was comfortable visualizing Leanna having intercourse with her new partner Rich. However, he became enraged when he visualized her having oral sex with Rich. He realized that he considered fellatio as extremely intimate experience and asked her to keep that exclusive to their relationship.

Jessica found the entire visualization pretty neutral, until she got to the part where, after having sex, her husband Will talked to the new woman about his feelings for her. She realized that she didn't mind her partner having sex with another woman, but felt extremely threatened by him having an intimate conversation with her.

The Jealousy Workbook

Chapter Five:

Freud's Jealousy Nightmare Scenario

Sigmund Freud is famous for inventing psychoanalysis, but he also had some very useful insights into jealousy and why it can be so painful and overwhelming. He described what he called the four major components of jealousy, a nightmarish combination of experiences that he believed occurred sequentially:

1. First, we experience *grief*, the terrible pain of actually losing or being afraid of losing someone we love.

2. Next, we are flooded with the very distressing *realization* that we cannot have everything we want in life, and that we may lose our precious relationship or some valued component of the relationship.

3. Then we are gripped with feelings of *enmity* towards the successful rival who has won the love of our partner or who we fear will succeed in stealing our partner.

4. Last, we turn our *anger* on ourselves in a belief that our own inadequacies as a partner will cause our partner to leave us. We fear that we are inferior to a rival and that we will lose our lover, and that we deserve to be abandoned for a "better" partner.

So you can see from Freud's description that jealousy taps into our worst fears about loss, grief, deprivation, rejection, humiliation, and abandonment. It also confirms our insecurities about our own inadequacies as a partner, and our fears that we don't deserve to be loved. You can learn something about your own jealousy by studying the four aspects he identified and assessing how strongly you experience each one, and which part is most painful and debilitating for you.

Exercise Six: Learn something from Sigmund Freud

Step One: Rate each component on a scale of one to ten, on two criteria:

Grief and loss: fear of losing your relationship

How large a part does this component play in your jealousy?

1____2____3____4____5____6____7____8____9____10____

How painful and debilitating is this component of your jealousy?

1____2____3____4____5____6____7____8____9____10____

Fear and sadness that we may not be able to have everything we want in this relationship and that we cannot control this situation

How large a part does this component play in your jealousy?

1____2____3____4____5____6____7____8____9____10____

How painful and debilitating is this component of your jealousy?

1____2____3____4____5____6____7____8____9____10____

Hostile feelings towards your "rival," the person who is having a relationship with your partner and who you fear will steal your beloved away from you

How large a part does this component play in your jealousy?

1____2____3____4____5____6____7____8____9____10____

How painful and debilitating is this component of your jealousy?

1____2____3____4____5____6____7____8____9____10____

Anger towards yourself for your perceived inadequacies as a partner, and a belief that your "rival" is in fact superior to you, so that you deserve to be abandoned for this other person.

How large a part does this component play in your jealousy?

1____2____3____4____5____6____7____8____9____10____

How painful and debilitating is this component of your jealousy?

1____2____3____4____5____6____7____8____9____10____

Step Two: Evaluate the accuracy of your ratings

Looking at the numbers you checked above, did any of these four components receive numbers over 5 in both categories? Any component that rates extremely high, either in playing a large part in your overall jealousy or in being intensely painful, or both, is clearly the place to start in confronting your jealousy.

Example: Zachary checked "9" in both categories for component number 4, because his most overpowering experience with jealousy was self-hatred. He explained, "I was judging myself to be a total loser, who any woman would dump immediately if she had anyone else to date." Just saying it out loud made him realize how inaccurate his belief was: he currently had a successful long-term relationship with his partner, who had dated numerous other men over the years and never left him for any of them. In trying to understand why he felt so bad about himself, he thought about his childhood competition with his older brother, who excelled in sports and had lots of women pursuing him in high school. Zachary was shy, "kind of a goth geek," didn't have a girlfriend until he was eighteen, and felt very insecure about his sexual attractiveness. However, since then, he had very positive experiences with women and had many women interested in relationships with him, so he had plenty of evidence that his old "script" about being a "loser" was untrue. Gradually, his self-esteem improved as he was able to remind himself that he no longer was competing with his brother, and that his current relationship was secure.

Another example: Alexis found that Freud's second component of jealousy was her Waterloo. She checked 10 in both categories for Number 2: "Fear and sadness that we may not be able to have everything we want in this relationship and that we cannot control this situation." She said, "Freud really had my number!" Her husband Jason tended to dismiss her requests for poly agreements, insisting on having complete freedom to do whatever he wanted in outside romantic relationships, no matter how much it hurt Alexis. She felt powerless, disrespected, and unloved. In couples counseling, I explained to Jason that he had confused an open marriage with being single. When you are single, you can sleep with anyone, spend as much time with anyone as you want to, and have whatever types of relationships you want to have with as many lovers as you can handle. When you are in a committed relationship, however, you must collaborate with your partner or spouse to negotiate some guidelines for outside relationships. He eventually "got it" that he could not have all the power in the marriage, and that some boundaries were appropriate in a poly relationship. He agreed to limit the number of outside lovers to a maximum of two at any one time, and to spend no more than three nights a week away from home. Alexis was comfortable with this compromise and gradually found her jealousy subsiding, since she felt more in control of how things were unfolding. She felt more secure about having enough of her husband's time and attention.

Step Three: What if you score high in more than one jealousy component?

Some people find that they have high numbers in two or more of Freud's four jealousy components. This means your jealousy is complicated, as it is being concurrently triggered by more than one variable. Usually, it's a sign that both you and your partner are contributing to the problem and that you both probably need to look at your beliefs and behavior in order to solve it. Here are some of the diverse factors that could be at work:

If you scored very high on all four jealousy components:

You may have a relationship history of being betrayed by a previous partner who repeatedly broke relationship agreements, or a partner who lied to you or abandoned you. It makes perfect sense that if you have had this history of distrust and deception, you would fear losing your partner, feel out of control, and experience a lot of anger towards your partner, their other partner, and yourself. Your first step towards reducing your jealousy is to assess whether or not your current partner is likely to betray you, or whether you are punishing them unfairly by projecting your past partner's bad behavior onto your current relationship. If your partner is in fact trustworthy, honest, and generally keeps their agreements, your suspicions are based on the past relationship. You may need some counseling or other support to feel more trusting.

If you scored very high on jealousy components 2 and 3:

Your current relationship may have started out as a monogamous relationship where your partner "cheated," then later negotiated for an open relationship. It's natural that you would feel a loss of control and experience a lot of anger towards your partner, their other partner, and yourself. Couples counseling and other support can help you work together as a couple to rebuild the trust you have lost.

If you scored very high on jealousy components 1 and 2:

Your current partner may have unrealistic expectations about your ability to handle their polyamorous behavior, or may be pushing you to move too quickly to accept their outside sexual relationships. This pushing can trigger fears that your partner will leave you if you don't agree to whatever relationship guidelines they want, and feeling coerced into something makes you feel disempowered. No one likes being pressured into going too far outside their comfort zone, and each person moves at a different pace. Your partner may need to give you more reassurance that they are committed to your relationship and that they will not leave you. Both you and your partner must be willing to make some compromises in order to meet your needs for security and abundance, as well as your partner's needs in their other relationships.

If you scored very high on jealousy components 1 and 4:

You may be struggling with shyness, deficits in interpersonal or communication skills, or low self-esteem. Naturally, these issues might make you more frightened of losing your partner's love, and might cause you to blame yourself and your perceived inadequacies as a partner. You may benefit from counseling, a support group, or workshops to improve your relationship skill-set and enhance your self-confidence. It is also possible that your partner is inadvertently undermining your emotional safety and self-esteem by being too critical, not demonstrating their love and appreciation for you, or by dismissing your concerns.

If you scored very high on jealousy components 1, 2, and 4:

You may be seeking a different model of open relationship than your partner, and those models may not be compatible. These mismatched expectations prevent you from getting what you want in this relationship, and cause distress that you cannot control the situation. Becoming aware of these conflicts creates fear of losing your relationship and cause you to blame yourself for not being able to make the relationship work. For instance, many open relationships are organized around the Primary-Secondary Model: a primary couple relationship is prioritized, and all other relationships are considered secondary to the initial couple. However, someone may fall in love with their secondary partner, and want their spouse to accept that relationship as a primary relationship. The primary partner may feel betrayed by this sudden change, and may not be able to adapt their model to fit this new reality. Couples counseling may be helpful in resolving this crisis, but some people will only be happy if they can be the "alpha" relationship.

> **An example:** James is a single man involved with Barbara, a married woman in an open relationship. James started out enjoying this casual fling, but rapidly became intensely involved with Barbara and wanted to become primary partners and move in with her and her family. She declined, saying that she was very fond of him but that she only had time for one primary relationship, and that her husband and kids had to come first.

So Sigmund Freud may not have known anything about polyamory, but his advice on jealousy can be useful to us today! He viewed jealousy as a nightmare driven by our worst fears of inferiority, humiliation, failure, loss, and abandonment. While delving into these primal fears can be extremely uncomfortable, it can be instrumental in understanding and managing our jealousy.

·

Chapter Six:

Is your jealousy rational?

You may encounter situations where you feel extremely jealous, but feel uncertain about whether these feelings are based on reality or on exaggerated fears. This chapter will help you discover whether your jealousy is rational, or whether perhaps you are overreacting or your imagination is running away with you. This exercise is called "The Jealousy Filter," because you are screening your jealousy by being a detective and asking yourself four questions to clarify the basis for your jealousy. For your jealousy to be firmly founded on a realistic fear of some type of loss, all four of these prerequisites must be true. This exercise can be used to learn more about your jealousy in advance of any problem, but it can also be used during an acute jealousy episode.

Exercise Seven: Your Jealousy Filter

Think of a time when you were intensely jealous, and put your jealousy through these four prerequisites. Were all four of these statements true at that time?

- You have access to a very valuable resource – the time, attention, affection, love, loyalty, priority, or sexual attention from a partner – but you fear losing it to someone else. ☐ yes ☐ no

- Another person wants that same resource from your partner. ☐ yes ☐ no

- You believe yourself to be in direct competition with that other person to get what you want, and you believe here is not enough of this resource for both of you to get what you want. ☐ yes ☐ no

- You believe that if push comes to shove, you will lose this contest and your competitor will win out. In other words, you will be compared to your rival and found inadequate, they will be seen as superior and/or more desirable, and they will walk away with the prize: the time, attention, affection, love, loyalty, priority, or sexual attention of your partner. ☐ yes ☐ no

An example:

You feel intensely jealous when you see an attractive person flirting with your partner at a party. Are all four prerequisites met?

- The first condition is true: you have a committed relationship but you fear losing it.

- The second prerequisite is not true, because you have no idea if this other person wants a relationship with your partner of if they are just flirting for the fun of it, to test their attractiveness, or to make their partner jealous.

- The third condition is not met, either, because you cannot say with any certainty whether they want your partner or whether your partner is interested in them. And even if the two of them do get involved romantically, there is no evidence that that would create a scarcity, that there is not enough for you both to get what you want.

- And the fourth condition is certainly not met, because there is no reason to believe that your partner would abandon you for this other person they have just met.

    Your jealousy fails the "reality check" and you may need to take a closer look at your insecurities and why they are being triggered by harmless flirting.

The Jealousy Workbook

Another example: Your partner has been telling you for several months that they are not happy with the relationship, and they have begun spending more time with another lover. When your partner tells you they want to go on a trip to Spain for a month with the other lover, this triggers a strong jealousy reaction.

Are all four prerequisites met?

- Prerequisite #1: Yes, you have a relationship and you fear losing it.

- Prerequisite #2: Yes, another person is taking up more and more of your partner's time, loyalty, and attention, and clearly wants that same resource.

- Prerequisite #3: Yes, you are in fact in direct competition with someone else who is able to persuade your partner to go on a long trip overseas, and there is good reason to believe that you and this other lover cannot both get what you want.

- And Prerequisite #4: Yes, since you partner has been expressing unhappiness in your relationship for quite some time, you are in danger of potentially losing your partner to someone else. Your jealousy is clearly based in reality, and you would be wise to ask your partner to go with you to couples counseling to work on your relationship.

This exercise can be very useful in helping you get a more realistic view of your jealous feelings and experiences. It helps take your jealousy out of the realm of insecurity and fears and into the realm of what is actually going on and what is most likely to happen. Instead of letting your imagination run away with your catastrophic fears of impending doom, you can test the validity of your fears and see if your concerns are valid and corrective action is needed, or if self-soothing and supportive responses might be more useful.

PART TWO:

Effective Interventions for Jealousy

The first part of this book was designed to help you understand your jealousy and prepare for situations which are likely to trigger jealousy. This next part is designed to help you when you are already feeling jealous. While many of these techniques can be "practiced" in advance to help you get a better handle on your jealousy, they are primarily for use when you are in the midst of a jealousy episode and need help immediately.

Chapter Seven:

Your jealousy pie chart

Frequently I receive phone calls from people in the midst of a jealousy crisis who shout into the phone, "Oh my god, I feel sooo jealous!!!" When I ask them what they are feeling, they just repeat, "I feel jealous!"

In fact, jealousy is not a single emotion, but a whole bundle of feelings, thoughts, sensations, memories, associations, and experiences that tend to get lumped together.

This first exercise will help you identify the essential components of your jealousy. It may seem complicated, and it does take some time and effort, but each step is useful in understanding your jealousy and responding to it effectively.

Exercise Eight: What are you actually feeling, thinking, and experiencing when you are jealous?

Step One: Identify your jealousy symptoms

Jealousy can include any or all of the feelings, thoughts, or sensations listed below.

Read over this list carefully. After each word or phrase, on a scale of 0 to 10, circle the number that best represents how intensely you experience each one during an acute jealousy episode. Each one that you rate at a 5 or above needs further attention.

- anger and rage 1 2 3 4 5 6 7 8 9 10
- fear and even terror 1 2 3 4 5 6 7 8 9 10
- betrayal 1 2 3 4 5 6 7 8 9 10
- anxiety or panic 1 2 3 4 5 6 7 8 9 10
- physical, mental and/or emotional agitation 1 2 3 4 5 6 7 8 9 10
- obsessive thoughts 1 2 3 4 5 6 7 8 9 10
- sadness and hurt 1 2 3 4 5 6 7 8 9 10
- exaggerated or catastrophic worries 1 2 3 4 5 6 7 8 9 10
- depression or sadness 1 2 3 4 5 6 7 8 9 10
- loneliness 1 2 3 4 5 6 7 8 9 10
- envy 1 2 3 4 5 6 7 8 9 10
- coveting 1 2 3 4 5 6 7 8 9 10
- self-loathing 1 2 3 4 5 6 7 8 9 10
- powerlessness 1 2 3 4 5 6 7 8 9 10
- feeling left out or excluded 1 2 3 4 5 6 7 8 9 10
- embarrassment and humiliation 1 2 3 4 5 6 7 8 9 10
- grief and loss 1 2 3 4 5 6 7 8 9 10
- fears of inadequacy 1 2 3 4 5 6 7 8 9 10
- feeling numb 1 2 3 4 5 6 7 8 9 10
- fatigue 1 2 3 4 5 6 7 8 9 10
- confusion and disorientation 1 2 3 4 5 6 7 8 9 10

- memory loss and difficulty concentrating 1 2 3 4 5 6 7 8 9 10
- feeling disrespected or mistreated 1 2 3 4 5 6 7 8 9 10
- difficulty sleeping. 1 2 3 4 5 6 7 8 9 10
- stomach cramps, nausea, vomiting, and/or diarrhea . . 1 2 3 4 5 6 7 8 9 10
- heart palpitations or pounding heartbeat 1 2 3 4 5 6 7 8 9 10
- shortness of breath or feelings of suffocation 1 2 3 4 5 6 7 8 9 10
- muscle aches and pains 1 2 3 4 5 6 7 8 9 10
- flu-like symptoms. 1 2 3 4 5 6 7 8 9 10
- dizziness and fainting 1 2 3 4 5 6 7 8 9 10
- being flooded with repetitive, painful memories 1 2 3 4 5 6 7 8 9 10
- revenge fantasies. 1 2 3 4 5 6 7 8 9 10
- paranoid beliefs 1 2 3 4 5 6 7 8 9 10
- compulsive behaviors 1 2 3 4 5 6 7 8 9 10

Any of these feelings, thoughts, or experiences can be intensified by past experiences which may be triggering your jealousy, whether or not those past experiences involved a romantic relationship. These experiences may be from childhood, such as feeling abandoned by a parent due to divorce, being neglected by a parent due to a parent's alcoholism or being self-absorbed, having a close friend move away and feeling alone, or feeling left out or inadequate due to a sibling getting more attention or being more successful in some way. Or a jealousy experience can be triggered by a more recent event in adulthood, such as a former lover leaving you for someone else, or being neglected by a former partner because of their involvement in their career or their commitment to other partners.

I have worked with clients who were suddenly flooded with jealous feelings, thoughts, and sensations due to a wide variety of non-relationship events: feeling outraged at being fired from a job despite hard work and talent, or devastated by the death of a parent who left more money to a sibling in their will, or feeling wounded when a daughter chose to have her stepfather walk her down the aisle at her wedding, or filled with envy when a band-mate got a solo recording contract.

All these experiences will tend to sensitize an individual to jealousy. Future circumstances may create a post-traumatic stress-type reaction based on those very painful past experiences. You can get a better handle on your jealousy if you study your past experiences to see what situations are most likely to trigger you, and what types of jealousy you are most likely to experience.

Step Two: Fear, anger, and sadness: the three primary jealousy symptoms

To better understand your jealousy, start with identifying your most prominent and consistent jealous feelings. The three primary negative emotions that humans can experience are fear, anger, and sadness – or, at their most extreme, terror, rage, and despair. While there are literally hundreds of feelings and emotions in the human arsenal, most of the negative ones fit into one of those three broader categories.

Most people experience some combination of fear, anger, and sadness when they have an intense jealousy reaction, but for most people, one of those three primary emotions is more prominent and more painful than the other two. Look again at which jealousy symptoms you identified in Step One, above, especially any that you rated at a 5 or above. Do most of those fall into the category of fear, anger, or sadness, or are all three part of your jealousy pie chart?

My anecdotal experience with people in open relationships indicates that women are more likely to identify fear or sadness as the predominant emotions of jealousy, but men are much more likely to experience anger as the primary symptom when they feel jealous.

Some studies have come to similar conclusions. In *The Evolution of Desire*, evolutionary biologist David Bussey writes that men are physiologically wired for angry responses to jealousy. He theorized that in the ancient past, this anger had a survival benefit in scaring away rival males and keeping a man's mate from defecting to another man. Bussey also believes that jealous anger in women did not create a positive outcome, so women evolved a different adaptation to jealousy. Whether or not his biological theories make any sense in the twenty-first century, my personal and professional experience concurs that jealous men tend to get angry and jealous women are more likely to experience fear or sadness.

Regardless of the cause or effect, you can make your jealousy more manageable by recognizing which of these three is most important for you, and zeroing in on problem-solving strategies specific to that emotion. Try this exercise to identify the percentages of these three primary negative emotions in your personal jealousy profile.

Exercise Nine: Draw your jealousy pie chart

1. Take a piece of paper and draw a large circle, a pie chart.

2. Remember the last time you experienced intense jealousy.

3. Imagine that your jealousy is inside this circle or pie chart, and ask yourself whether you were feeling more fear, anger, or sadness while you were jealous. If you have trouble differentiating between these primary emotions, look over the list above of all the emotions that jealousy can include, and try to identify which things on that list you are experiencing. Then take those feelings and try to determine whether they fall into the category of fear, anger, or sadness.

4. Write inside the circle on the left side the name of whichever of those three emotions was most intense, and make your best guess about what percentage of the pie chart that emotion filled up.

5. Think about the other two primary emotions, and write each one of them inside the circle, with the percentage of the jealousy pie chart that they occupy for you.

The percentages should add up to approximately 100%. If they don't, you could benefit from going over the pie chart again and seeing if there is some part that you have overlooked. If the percentages add up to more than 100%, that probably means that all three emotions feel quite intense for you. In that case, it can be useful to think about all three and try to determine if any one of them is more painful or bigger than the other two.

General example: A woman who drew this pie chart remembered that whenever she was jealous, her jealousy was 50% fear and 20% anger. She couldn't quite figure out what was in the other 30%. After studying the list above, she identified the rest of her jealousy as 10% feeling powerless, 15% feeling betrayed by her partner, and 5% feeling lonely and alone. Feeling powerless and lonely fall into the realm of sadness, so she wrote "Sadness: 20%" in the pie chart, and her feelings of betrayal were angry feelings, so she added that 15% to the anger quotient in the circle. So her final pie chart showed 50% fear, 35% anger, and 15% sadness. This allowed her to focus primarily on her fears, which made up at least half of her jealousy, and then on her anger, which was the other big piece.

Personal example: When you think about a recent intense jealousy episode, you remember feeling enraged and even fantasizing about driving to your partner's other boyfriend's house to pound on the door and scream at him. You also remember feeling obsessed by fears that he may be better in bed than you, and feelings of inferiority because he is more affluent and has been taking your partner to expensive restaurants and to the opera. Because you are part of a tight-knit gay community and some of your friends tend to gossip, you worry that he might be looking down on you, and that your friends may be talking about you and making fun of you. You identify anger as the primary emotion you are feeling, and write in the pie chart: "Anger, 75%." In looking at these other fears about his money and his sexual prowess, you write "Fear: 15%." Thinking about your concerns about the public humiliation of him looking down on you or your loss of status in your friends' eyes, you notice feeling despair, and write in the pie chart: "Sadness: 10 %."

Chapter Eight:

How to manage the fear, anger, and sadness of jealousy

Now that you have an idea of the general percentages of fear, anger, and sadness that make up your jealousy, what can you do about it? Start with the one primary emotion that is the strongest and most distressing, and learn more about it, so you can develop better coping strategies.

Exercise Ten: Fear

If you identified fear as the predominant emotion, with a higher percentage than anger or sadness, ask yourself these three questions and write down the answers:

Question #1: What am I afraid of?

Dr. Ayala Pines is a psychologist who has done extensive research on jealousy and has written several books on the subject. In her amazing book, *Romantic Jealousy: Causes, Symptoms, and Cures*, she identifies The Five Cardinal Fears of Jealousy:

1. Fear of abandonment ("He's going to leave me for someone else")

2. Losing face and losing status in the community ("How could she humiliate me by telling our friends about sleeping with him?")

3. Betrayal ("I just can't believe he would hurt me like this!")

4. Competitiveness and fear of our own inadequacy ("I wonder if her new lover is better in bed than me!")

5. Envy towards our partner's other partner ("If only I were as attractive/smart/successful/rich/etc. as he is!")

I would add to Dr. Pines' Five Cardinal Fears of Jealousy:

6. Fear of scarcity and deprivation ("I'll be lonely and unsatisfied because he'll be too distracted and busy and with her!")

Because Dr. Pines' work is focused on romantic jealousy in monogamous relationships, there is one very powerful cardinal fear that is not mentioned in her research: fear of scarcity or deprivation, a fear that is much more relevant and important in open relationships. If your spouse develops an outside relationship, they will take some of their time, loyalty, attention, sex, and other resources that have previously been directed to you, and divert them to the other partner. This could leave you with a net loss and an experience of scarcity, feeling that you are not getting enough to feel satisfied.

In looking over this list of six fears, which one or ones are you most afraid of when you are experiencing fear during a jealousy attack? Write them down in the order of importance, with the most painful and intense fear first.

Question #2: How likely is it that my fear will come true? And even if the likelihood is slim, is there some kernel of truth in my fear? And if it does come true, how will I handle it?

Question #3: What do I need to do to address this fear? What can I do to take care of myself, and what kind of support can I ask for from my partner, friends, and community, in order to resolve this fear?

A general example:

Question #1: Whenever Jennifer's lover Peter had a date with his new partner Melanie, Jennifer feared he would find Melanie more attractive and interesting and would end their long-term relationship. In examining her fears, this was her most intense, terrifying feeling during jealousy episodes, and she was obsessed with anxiety that she would be abandoned and alone.

Question #2: When she asked herself how likely this was to come true, she had to admit that Peter had had three other lovers in the past and had never left her for any of them, so it seemed unlikely that he would leave her for this new one. However, she did find a kernel of truth in her fear, because one previous outside relationship had caused so much conflict between them that they almost had broken up over it. She realized that a big part of her fear of abandonment was coming from her memories of those painful arguments over the previous girlfriend, and how close they had come to breaking up at that time. Since they had not had nearly as much conflict over Melanie, and her partner was showing no signs of actually wanting to leave her, she felt calmer and more secure about her relationship. And when she thought of how she could cope if in fact her worst fear did come true and he left her, she reminded herself that she had been single for two years before meeting her partner, and she was quite happy then – so if they did break up, she would survive it.

Question #3: When she asked herself what she needed to handle this fear, she decided to ask Peter to limit his dates with Melanie to once or twice a week. He had been generally only seeing her once a week, but ironically Melanie had become very insecure about the relationship and had been asking for more time with Peter as reassurance of his interest in her. Peter agreed that he would have one overnight date with Melanie and one lunch date during the week, when Jennifer was at work and would be too busy to obsess about them having a date. Peter also agreed not to email or text Melanie during his dates with Jennifer, as that made Jennifer feel insulted and ignored. Instead he would text and email Melanie a few times during the workday when it would not intrude on his time with Jennifer. This way Melanie would get enough contact with him but Jennifer would not be triggered with fears of abandonment. Jennifer also agreed to make dates with friends or get involved in some other activity on the one night a week that Peter would be with Melanie. This way she would be preoccupied with doing something fun, rather than sitting home alone feeling anxious and jealous.

Exercise Eleven: Anger

If you identified anger as the predominant emotion, with a higher percentage than fear or sadness, ask yourself these four questions and write down the answers:

Question #1: Who or what am I angry at? Am I angry at my partner, at my partner's other partner(s), at myself, at someone else altogether? Am I angry at a situation or circumstance rather than at a particular person, or am I angry that something is out of my control?

Question #2: Is my anger based in the current situation, or is it being triggered by somethng in my past, or am I angry about something I fear is going to happen as a result of the current situation? Is there a rational basis for my anger, and if so, does the anger seem proportional to the situation? On a scale of 1 to 10, how angry do I feel about this situation? Is that number appropriate, and if not, what number would be reasonable? And even if my anger does not really seem justified, is there some valid reason I feel mistreated or disrespected?

Question #3: What is the grievance that I want to redress? Being angry is usually a response to a feeling that someone has not behaved appropriately in relation to us, or that something is unfair or unethical. So it may be useful to identify the specific action or experience that has made you feel victimized in some way. State as clearly as possible what you feel is wrong with this situation, and what you believe would be the correct behavior or outcome.

Question #4: What do I need to do to address, express, and/or let go of this anger? What can I do to take care of myself, and what kind of support can I ask for from my partner, friends, and community, in order to resolve this?

A general example:

Jamal and his wife Maria made plans to go to his parents' house for dinner, but she accidentally scheduled that same evening to take their kids to the movies with her lover Raquel and Raquel's kids. Jamal became extremely angry at Maria for carelessly double-booking the date and he felt very uncomfortable having to call his parents and cancel the dinner.

Question #1: Jamal felt angry that his only other choice would have been to tell the kids they had to miss the movie and their fun plans, and that Maria had put him in the position of "being the bad guy." So he was angry at both Maria and at the "no-win" situation. He also realized he was furious at Raquel, even though he could not really explain why. He also felt angry at himself for "being lazy" and letting Maria be in charge of the family's social calendar, telling himself that if he had been more on top of things, he would have realized that there was a conflict.

Question #2: He decided that his anger at Maria was justified, because she could have prevented this scheduling conflict. He rated his anger towards her at 7 on a scale of 1 to 10. However, she reminded him that several times in the past, he had canceled dates with her at the last minute because his boyfriend had come into town unexpectedly, and that she had been gracious about that. In thinking it over, he decided that being angry at about a 3 or 4 rather than a 7 would be more proportional to the situation. Maria had given him enough advance notice of the snafu that he was able to reschedule with his parents a week in advance, and they had not been inconvenienced. He realized that his anger at Raquel was not justified, but that he was holding on to some anger towards her from an unrelated issue: Raquel had recently offered to take care of their kids so they could go away for the weekend to celebrate their fifteenth wedding anniversary, but that she had not followed up on actually committing to a specific weekend.

Question #3: Jamal decided that his grievance was that he felt Maria's behavior showed disregard for him and disrespect for his parents. In writing that down and then communicating it to Maria, he realized that she meant no disrespect – it was simply an error due to the stress of keeping track of the kids' schedules, her work schedule, etc., rather than a deliberate insult. As a result, he was able to let go of that part of the anger. His other grievance was that he now felt distrustful of Maria's ability to juggle her marriage and her relationship with Raquel.

Question #4: He asked Maria for reassurance that she would be more careful with scheduling in the future, and Maria promised to check with him before committing to weekend dates with Raquel that could interfere with family events. Jamal's boyfriend suggested that they use a version of an on-line Google calendar to track their family plans, individual work schedules, and outside dates, and they decided to try that to prevent future scheduling conflicts.

Exercise Twelve: Sadness

If you identified sadness as the predominant emotion, with a higher percentage than fear or anger, ask yourself these four questions and write down the answers:

Question #1: What are the sad emotions I am experiencing: feelings of depression, insecurity, inadequacy, self-loathing, boredom, loneliness, hurt, loss, grief, feeling overwhelmed, exhaustion, feeling debilitated, abandonment?

Question #2: What am I sad about? Is it a specific behavior of my partner that seems to have triggered this sadness, or simply the fact that they are having another relationship, or that they are attracted to someone else? What is it about this situation that seems to create sadness for me?

Question #3: Is my sadness based in the current situation, or being triggered by something in the past? Is there a rational basis for these sad feelings, and if so, does it seem proportional to the situation? On a scale of 1 to 10, how sad do I feel about this situation? Is that number appropriate, and if not, what number would be reasonable? And even if my sadness seems irrational, is there some valid reason I feel unhappy about this? What exactly is wrong with this situation, and what do I believe is the appropriate alternative or outcome?

Question #4: What do I need to do to address, express, and/or let go of this sadness? What can I do to take care of myself, and what kind of support can I ask for from my partner, friends, and community, in order to resolve this?

Example:

Question #1: Cathy had lived with her partner Janna for ten years in a monogamous relationship when they decided to explore an open relationship. But when Janna began a new relationship with another woman, Cathy was overwhelmed with depression and could not stop crying whenever she thought about it or whenever Janna had a date with her other girlfriend. When Cathy examined her intense feelings of sadness, she realized that she felt an overwhelming sense of loss, more than anything else.

Question #2: When asked why she felt such a sense of mourning, Cathy was able to identify that the end of the sexual and romantic exclusivity in her relationship felt like an irrevocable loss, which she described as "an earth-shattering change in the relationship" which filled her with sadness and made her cry. Suddenly everything else about the relationship felt "up for grabs," as if the security of the relationship was in jeopardy. She felt as if she was about to lose everything that mattered to her, including losing her partner to another woman. And she found herself mourning the natural cooling-off of intense passion in her relationship over the years, as she could see the contrast between this and the New Relationship Energy (NRE) Janna was experiencing in the new relationship.

The Jealousy Workbook

Question #3: In looking back into her past, she could see that her sadness was being triggered, not only by Janna's new romance, but by a past experience of a former gilrfriend leaving her for another woman. She knew she was projecting some of her pain from that past break-up onto Janna, when in fact the two situations were not really similar at all. On a scale of 1 to10, she rated her sadness at an 8, but could see that a more appropriate number was about a 5. She realized that she missed having more passion and romance with Janna. Seeing Janna getting dressed up and planning special romantic dates with her new girlfriend made her feel envious and left out, and she asked Janna to plan some exciting dates with her as well.

Question #4: Cathy and Janna started having weekly date nights and going out to hear bands at clubs, something they had loved doing when they first started dating. They also began writing each other sexy emails and texting each other with romantic messages, which helped Cathy feel she was receiving special, romantic attention, and feel more loved and desired. And she and Janna had a few long talks acknowledging that the loss of sexual exclusivity was in fact a much bigger loss than either of them had anticipated. However, they both felt that the positive gains from having an open relationship would compensate for this loss and add up to a net gain overall. Her sadness gradually subsided to a 2 or 3, which was much more manageable.

You can see from this exercise that it can be enlightening and helpful to go through the "nuts and bolts" of breaking down your jealousy and the feelings you are having. It can be challenging to be objective about whether your fears, anger and/or sadness have a basis in reality, or whether your insecurities or your imagination are running away with you.

Chapter Nine:

Jealousy, envy and coveting

When I work with clients on what they call jealousy issues, they frequently describe feelings that I would define, instead, as "envy." Envy happens when you see someone else having something you really want, and you feel a strong craving to have what they are experiencing.

How is envy different from coveting? The key difference between envy and other similar emotions is that you do not have a desire to take what they have away from them, you just wish you could have something like that, too. It is a wish to have something as valuable as what they have: having as much fun as they have, as much sex, as much romance, making as much money as they do, feeling as satisfied in life, having as much status as they do, as great a job as they do, wishing your kids were as talented and successful as theirs are, that you had a wonderful extended family like they do, or that you were as smart or gifted or charismatic or good-looking as they are.

"Coveting" is frequently confused with envy. Most people have heard the word from the Ten Commandments in the Old Testament: "Thou shalt not covet thy neighbor's wife." (While it is curious that these Commandments say nothing about coveting thy neighbor's husband, I suspect that this is also forbidden.) Coveting assumes that you not only want to sleep with your neighbor's wife but also steal her away from him. Envy would mean you think he is a really lucky guy to have such a fantastic wife, and you wish you could have a sexual relationship with her, too, or with someone just as wonderful as her.

Envy frequently crops up in many different forms in open relationships, and can be quite confusing. Sometimes it is difficult to know who we are envying, our partner or their other partner, or exactly what it is that we actually envy.

Some people have argued that envy is a component of jealousy. Others contend that it is a separate phenomenon, because it is not caused by your partner having another relationship but rather by you missing out on something you want to experience. Whichever theory you believe, you can get a better handle on your jealousy by teasing apart the envy experience and looking at it on its own. The good news about envy is that it is usually one of the easier components to solve, mainly because it is something over which you have more control.

Exercise Thirteen: Separating envy from jealousy

Step One: Clarify the emotions you are currently feeling

Sit quietly for a few moments. Think about the current situation that seems to be creating jealousy for you, and try to become aware of all your feelings and emotions related to this situation. Now, jot down a quick list of each feeling. You may want to look back at your "Jealousy Pie Chart" from the previous chapter, to clarify whether you are feeling more fear, anger, or sadness, and to further identify the nuances of your emotional experience of jealousy.

For example, what if your partner goes out for a hike in the wilderness and has passionate sex in the woods with their other lover? When you think about the emotions that fall into the "fear" category, you may fear being abandoned and replaced by someone else. Within the "sadness" category of emotions, you may feel lonely, crushed, and rejected. When you examine your "anger" feelings, thinking of your partner in the woods with another lover may make you feel betrayed and disrespected.

Step Two: Name that longing and identify the things you want

Looking at each of the feelings on your list, notice which ones are longings for things you want, and which are distressing emotions about things you don't want. The old adage says that people tend to move towards pleasure and away from pain. Some of your most intense emotions in this situation may be envy that your partner is having experiences that you long for yourself. For instance, you may be wistfully remembering the early days of your relationship ,when your partner would whisk you away for a day of romantic trysts, and wishing for a revival of that passion. Or you may be envious that your partner has some New Relationship Energy in their life right now, and wish you could be in such a happy mood as they seem to be. Or you may be envious of your partner's success in finding a new lover, when you are frustrated in meeting new people.

Or are you envious that your partner gets to go out and have fun while you are bored at work or stuck at home changing diapers or paying bills? Or do you envy your partner's new lover because you believe they are more appealing in some way than you are?

Step Three: Who and what do you envy?

Once you have been able to identify which of your feelings qualify as "envy," ask yourself if you are more envious of your partner, or of their other partner, or of an experience. If you discover you envy both of them, you may want to assign a percentage to each one. For instance, your envy may be about 60% towards your partner because they suddenly seem alive and infatuated and have become so self-confident, while 40% of your envy is towards their other partner because they work part-time and can go to nightclubs with your partner till 2:00 AM and then stay up all night having sex. You may also become aware that you don't envy either of them so much as you envy the activities they are involved in or the positive experiences they are having.

Step Four: Restrain yourself from shutting down their fun; pursue your own bliss instead

If you envy the camping trips, the concerts, the sexual experimentation, the emotional intimacy they are having, it may mean you need to indulge in some of those activities yourself rather than being angry at them for hogging all the fun. Often, the painful longing of envy causes people to demand that their partner stop seeing an outside lover or curtail the most satisfying elements of that relationship. If you can somehow see past your distress, it may be wiser to view your partner and their other relationship as role models for what you want to create in your own life. They have stumbled onto something wonderful. Rather than taking that away from them, try to stretch yourself and realize that you can have something just as good, or even better, by pursuing the things that make you happy.

That goal could take many forms: stepping up your efforts to find a satisfying outside relationship of your own, rekindling the passion in your primary relationship and prioritizing quality time together, and/or taking time for doing things you love or enhancing your own life in other ways.

Some examples:

Janelle and Ricardo are a cohabiting heterosexual couple. When Janelle started a relationship with Douglas, a somewhat younger guy who was a professional dancer, Ricardo experienced intense emotional pain, which he found very difficult to explain. With counseling, he began to realize he was extremely envious of both Janelle and Douglas, but for very different reasons. He was envious of Janelle because she was experiencing a giddy infatuation and increased self-esteem. He had been trying to find other partners, but had been "striking out" after going on dates with several women, who all rejected him because he was married and they were looking for a primary relationship. He was longing for exactly the type of excitement and romance she was experiencing, and he was sincerely happy for her and did not want her to stop seeing Douglas. But he envied her having a hot love affair while he was feeling very left out and alone. And because Ricardo had given up a career as an actor in order to become a paralegal to support his family, he envied Douglas having a career making good money as a dancer in music videos with famous hip-hop stars. Janelle showed him a picture of Douglas, and he became even more envious of his young, sexy, muscular body, since Ricardo was beginning to feel middle-aged and dumpy. Douglas helped solve the problem by fixing Ricardo up on a date with Allison, who was also a dancer, and they began a passionate love relationship. Once Ricardo was enjoying some of the same NRE and feeling more sexually desirable, his envy subsided.

Vanessa, Rena, and Althea are a lesbian triad that has been living together for five years. While Vanessa was pregnant with their first child, she was quite ill with morning sickness and was too sick and exhausted to enjoy sex. She told Rena and Althea to have sex without her as often as they pleased, but whenever they did, she became sullen and had crying spells. At first she attributed it to the hormonal mood swings of pregnancy, and then she thought she was having an acute jealousy episode, but eventually realized that she was feeling intense envy towards both of her lovers. She listened wistfully to the moans and cries of her two partners making love in the other bedroom, wishing she felt well enough to join them. Because she had previously had a very passionate sexual relationship with both Rena and Althea, she missed that intimacy so much that she felt depressed when they would excuse themselves to go to bed together. When she explained her dilemma, Rena suggested that Vanessa come into the bed with them for cuddling and kisses even if she did not feel sexual. The next few times they wanted to make love, they persuaded Vanessa to join them, and she felt much less envious because she was given lots of affection and attention and felt included.

Chapter Ten:

Two approaches for managing jealousy: the engineering model and the phobia model

There are two basic approaches for managing jealousy, which I call the engineering model and the phobia model. They are not mutually exclusive and many people use some aspects of both models. The engineering model is an attempt to identify what situations and behaviors trigger your jealousy, and to try to "engineer" those triggers out of your life by making agreements to avoid those specific situations. The phobia model attempts to gradually expose yourself to each of the things that trigger your jealousy, to take the emotional charge out of the situation with repeated experience.

Exercise Fourteen: Will the engineering approach or the phobia model work best for you?

Step One: Jealousy requires trial and error

Neither approach is a simple and easy solution to jealousy. Expect some "bumps" as you experiment to discover what works for your relationship. Jealousy can bring up many powerful feelings and unpredictable emotions, so be gentle with yourself and your partner, and don't expect too much too fast. Start by expressing your own needs and desires to your partner, and asking them to tell you what agreements would be ideal for them in any open relationship. Try to balance each person's needs and limits.

Step Two: Share the power when making agreements

Create a "win-win" situation by giving each person as much voice as possible in decisions and rule-making. No one should try to bully their partner into going along with a relationship agreement that does not feel safe. On the other hand, no one should feel trapped by an agreement that is too restrictive. Be willing to compromise, within reason, to make sure everyone's needs are met as much as possible. If one person is arbitrarily making decisions and refusing to respect a partner's requests, couples counseling or mediation may help establish a better power balance in the relationship.

Step Three: How much do you need predictability?

Individuals vary significantly in how much they need to be able to predict what will happen in their lives, and this is especially true in an open relationship. Many people feel much safer if they know that their partner will be following specific rules and guidelines when developing outside relationships with other lovers. A very common statement I hear quite often is, "I don't deal well with surprises." Many people find that not knowing exactly what to expect from their partner regarding any outside relationships creates intolerable anxiety and distress. If this level of predictability is important to you, you probably will benefit from using the engineering model for managing jealousy, at least for now.

Most people find that they need more rules and guidelines when they first explore an open relationship. This creates a safe container for trying something new and complex, giving them more of an idea what to expect, controlling some of the variables, and reducing the amount of painful stimuli to manage. However, over time, many people discover that they can cope with more flexibility and fewer rules as it becomes more clear what guidelines are actually necessary.

Step Four: How much do your trust your partner's judgment (as well as your own)?

This question is not meant to imply that you or your partner are not trustworthy. It is meant to acknowledge that both of you are learning a new set of skills and taking a leap of faith into the unknown.

One client told her partner, "I know you are honest and have great integrity. But I wouldn't trust you to fly an airplane, because you have no training or experience to do it, and I don't know how either of us will do with polyamory because neither of us have ever done it before and we have no idea what the hell we are doing yet."

In an open relationship, you are trusting yourself and your partner to make the right decisions under new and extremely difficult conditions. For instance, it's asking a lot of anyone to prioritize their partner's needs and make appropriate decisions while under the influence of lust, passion, projection, romantic delusions, and infatuation (and sometimes alcohol or drugs). We are asking our partner to be completely rational and choose the higher path when that may mean overriding their own intense primal needs for sex, love, attention, validation, and intimacy. This takes practice, and both you and your partner will be on a steep learning curve.

My experience is that most people will make a few errors in judgment, which they will immediately regret. These mistakes may damage their partner's trust and take time and effort to repair. I am not excusing bad behavior, but rather recognizing that even a person with impeccable integrity can be vulnerable to making a mistake in a very charged situation involving sex and romance. Be prepared to forgive a less than perfect performance as you both develop better skills. Most people do not make the same mistake twice, after seeing the terrible pain they have inadvertently inflicted on their partner and having to clean up the mess they have caused in their relationship.

Using the engineering model usually reduces the number of disastrous mistakes in the beginning of an open relationship. This is true for two reasons:

1. Having clear guidelines makes it less likely that your partner will misunderstand what you expect of them, and less likely that they will do something that will hurt you. Frequently, when couples do not have explicit rules, one partner says, "I can't believe you thought it was okay to have sex with my best friend!" And the partner will answer, "But you never told me she was off-limits! How could I have known you would be upset?" Many couples counseling sessions start off with an irate spouse shouting, " I assumed you would know better than to do _____!" and the partner responding, "I had not idea that you didn't want me to do _____." Assuming your partner shares your list of acceptable behaviors is fairly likely to lead to disaster.

2. In the heat of a passionate moment, it is common for someone to become confused about what is acceptable to their partner, or to convince themselves that it is okay to do something that they suspect may hurt their partner. Talking over specific boundaries and making agreements ahead of time makes people less likely to "forget" or get fuzzy-brained at a crucial decision point.

While many couples choose to have a lot of boundaries when they start an open relationship, as time goes on, they may choose to drop a lot of these rules. This is partly because they feel more trusting of their partner's ability and commitment to handle things well. In addition, they have seen through experience that their partner can have other relationships while remaining loyal to them and not abandoning them.

Step Five: How important are freedom and autonomy to you?

While agreeing on some rules makes most people feel safer, some people feel suffocated by guidelines. Some people are motivated to explore an open relationship because they love the freedom to make their own choices about sex, love, and relationships. They chafe at being restricted by a list of do's and don'ts. If this is true for both you and your partner, you may have a strong preference for the phobia model of managing jealousy, rather than the engineering model of making agreements. Personal autonomy and having control over their lives is a key value for some people, and their relationship is enhanced by being able to give each other the gift of being allowed to pursue other relationships freely.

However, much more often, one partner's need for freedom is in conflict with their partner's need for security. People who have autonomy as a major value may find it difficult to stick with boundaries and guidelines that allow their partner to feel comfortable. When one partner wants more freedom and the other needs more boundaries, they can become locked in a power struggle where one partner refuses to agree to any rules and the other tries to exert more control over their partner's behavior. The only way out of this impasse is for both partners to be willing to compromise, by identifying the areas in which they can allow more freedom and the areas where limits are appropriate. If this sounds familiar, you can help your partner understand that this is not an attack on their needs by explaining that freedom is a core value for you.

Some couples find they do not have enough overlap to be compatible, because both partners are unhappy even when they are stretching themselves to accommodate their partner's needs. One partner will feel bullied and disrespected by having crucial boundaries violated, and the other will feel imprisoned by restrictions they can't accept. This can be a deal-breaker if there is not enough common ground.

The Jealousy Workbook

Control and freedom are not an either/or proposition. Anyone who enters any relationship is consenting to relinquish some amount of control, as any relationship involves negotiating time, activities, sharing space, privacy, agency, acceptable behaviors, etc. If you are single and unattached, you can have complete freedom to do whatever you want, with whoever you want, whenever you please. If you need this level of autonomy, it means you want to be single. If you want to be in a committed relationship, you and your partner must share the power and negotiate decisions about what behaviors you expect from each other, including how to pursue other sexual and romantic relationships.

Some successful examples of the engineering model:

George and Marsha were on the verge of breaking up because of George's secondary relationship with Barbara. Marsha realized that she got much more jealous when George saw Barbara on weekends: the new relationship upset her schedule, and she felt insulted that George was giving away his "prime time" to someone else. So she asked George to reserve weekends for her, and see Barbara only on weeknights. As soon as she was promised every weekend with George, her jealousy became much more manageable. After several months, she felt secure enough to give George permission to spend one weekend night with Barbara each week.

Bob and Peter are in a committed relationship. Bob wanted sex more often, so Peter told him to go to the baths and have anonymous sex with other men. However, he became withdrawn when Bob actually went out, and even less inclined to want sex. He was worried that Bob might have unsafe sex with other men and be exposed to HIV or other sexually transmitted infections. They agreed to be re-tested for HIV, and negotiated a clear agreement that they would use condoms in any penetrative sex outside of their relationship. Peter's jealousy subsided so much that he began asking Bob to tell him about his sexual adventures. This sharing brought them closer, and as a result they began having sex more frequently.

Beth and Mark had agreed to an open relationship, but Beth was very jealous when Mark told her that he wanted to start a relationship with Janet. Beth asked Mark and Janet to give her a month to get used to the idea before becoming sexually involved. As Beth got to know Janet, she decided that Mark had excellent taste in women, and she agreed to them having sex. The first few nights Mark spent with Janet, Beth couldn't sleep and was very frightened. But she waited it out and her jealousy faded. Because she had a voice in how things unfolded, and because her partner complied with her requests, her jealousy was minimized.

Jessica believed in open marriage, but she became very jealous when John initiated a sexual relationship with Carol. Jessica had already felt lonely and neglected for years because John was obsessed with his work and didn't give her enough time and enough sex. They made an explicit agreement that he would only spend two nights a week with Carol; the other five nights of the week, he would come home earlier from work and spend time with Jessica. As soon as John started spending more quality time with her, their intimacy was greatly enhanced, and her jealousy subsided.

The Jealousy Workbook

Exercise Fifteen: Using the phobia model for managing jealousy

A phobia is just an overreaction to a real danger. For instance, many people are afraid of flying in a plane – and in fact there is a real danger of a plane crash, but the likelihood is quite minuscule. Many people are afraid of swimming, and there is in fact a real danger of drowning, but the likelihood is small. Some people are phobic of snakes, and of course some snakes are deadly, so the fear is not entirely unfounded. Jealousy is a phobic response to a situation that could in fact pose a danger to your relationship, but your reaction is probably out of proportion to the reality of the actual risk.

Three components are central to the phobia model of managing jealousy:

Step One: Learn to accept jealousy as a normal but exaggerated response

It is natural to react with jealousy to your partner having other relationships, because this is a stressful, emotionally charged change in your life. Jealousy is not completely irrational, because there is always some risk involved in having outside relationships. However, you can reduce your phobia by recognizing that your reaction is excessive, and that you can probably safely turn down the volume on the jealousy. Assess the actual danger and develop a realistic picture. You may want to ask yourself these two questions:

1. What is the worst thing that could happen in this situation?, and

2. How likely is it that this will actually occur?

Most of the time, you will have overestimated the risk of a catastrophic outcome, such as losing your partner to another lover.

Step Two: Use systematic desensitization to gradually increase your tolerance for the situation that creates a phobic response

The most effective treatment for any type of phobia is called systematic desensitization. This means using an incremental approach to help people become more comfortable with the situation they fear. By gradually experiencing the situation that triggers the phobia, and by incrementally escalating that exposure, a person can slowly get used to something that was once terrifying, and can overcome their fears.

For instance, if someone is afraid of heights, they can pinpoint exactly what situations frighten them, and then gradually try to make those situations safe enough to tolerate. First, they might practice walking up a few flights of stairs every day for a week. Then, perhaps they would go up an escalator every day for a week or two. Once they felt they could tolerate those activities, they might try climbing a ladder, and eventually even going to the top of a hill or mountain. Gradually they would likely to be able to tolerate heights, and their fears would be reduced or eliminated.

This approach can help you manage jealous feelings. Using the three columns below, make a list of behaviors and situations that have triggered your jealousy. Group each item under mild jealousy, moderate jealousy, or severe jealousy. Then pick at least one item from the "mild jealousy" column and make a commitment to expose yourself to that situation or behavior in the near future. You can plan with your partner ways to minimize your discomfort and make the time and space for any aftercare you may need to recover after the experience. This could include being able to see or check in with your partner right afterward, planning something fun with a friend to distract yourself, etc. Once you develop the resilience and self-confidence to handle this item, you can gradually try all the things on the "mild" list. As your tolerance increases, you can move on to the "causes moderate jealousy" column, eventually feeling strong enough to tackle the situations listed under "causes severe jealousy." The goal is to become "desensitized" to these triggers by practicing them repeatedly until they no longer provoke the same level of distress.

Causes mild jealousy   Causes moderate jealousy   Causes severe jealousy

_____

_____

_____

_____

_____

An example:

Brent and John have lived together for twenty years. John has a long-time casual sex partner, Jason, who lives in a nearby city; they have dates once or twice a month when Jason is in town. John also likes to go to the baths for anonymous sex, and has recently started meeting other men through dating apps such as Scruff. To try to become more comfortable with John's activities, Brent decided to try the phobia model. First he wrote this list:

Causes mild jealousy

- John going to the baths for anonymous sex

- John spending time on his Smartphone looking for other guys to date on Scruff

- Hearing John calling his fuck-buddy Jason and making a date

Causes moderate jealousy

- John going out on a date with someone new
- John coming home after a date with Jason looking really happy
- Canceling plans with me to go on a date
- John staying out all night when he goes to the baths
- When John is too tired for sex because he was out late on a date

Causes severe jealousy

- If we didn't have enough time together because he was spending time with someone else
- If he fell in love with someone else
- If he got involved with a younger guy
- If he went out with someone else on the weekend instead of being with me

Brent realized that every item on the "severe jealousy" list were things that had never actually happened, but that were terrifying possibilities. He felt reassured that "my worst case scenario is not even likely to happen, so I decided to stop wasting time future-tripping, and just focus on what is actually happening." He talked with John and they made some plans for John to start with the activities on the "mild jealousy" list. John was happy to hear that Brent only felt mild jealousy when he went to the baths for sex. Brent explained that because it was so anonymous and would not result in any relationship, he didn't feel threatened. John had been careful to call Jason when Brent was not home, to avoid triggering jealousy, but Brent said he wanted to get used to hearing them set up dates. So they tried that a few times, with John telling him in advance that he was going to call Jason, so it wasn't a surprise, and Brent became much more comfortable with it. And they set up a few specific times when John could be on his phone on Scruff looking for dates, and Brent found that it was much easier for him if John told him if explicitly when he was just enjoying looking and when he was actually seeking a sex partner. They both felt more competent to manage these jealousy situations, and Brent said he felt like the "teamwork" of doing this together had brought them closer as a couple.

Step Three: Revisit the agreement after a specific time period, and fine-tune as needed

When using the phobia model and exposing yourself to a challenging jealousy situation, add some safety by agreeing to reevaluate the agreement after a specific time period. You might decide to try it for a month or six weeks, and set a date to revisit this decision with a discussion about how it is working and whether you both are comfortable with it. Often there is a need to fine-tune the agreement, as it is impossible to know in advance what parts will be hardest to manage. Be prepared to dial it back if you have gone too far, and try to be as flexible as possible. If things have gone smoothly during the trial period, decide whether you want to incorporate this into your relationship agreement or whether you want to try it out for a longer period to be certain that it will work in the long run.

A few examples of the phobia model in action:

Susan realized that she couldn't handle her husband Bill spending the night with his lover Rachel. She put that on her "causes moderate jealousy" list, but him spending a few evenings a week with Rachel was on her "mild jealousy list." So Bill agreed to come home every night, as long as he could spend a few evenings each week with Rachel. After a month, Susan was no longer so jealous, so he started spending one night a week with Rachel, with the caveat that if Susan got really jealous she could ask him to come home. After a few more months, she decided that it was okay for Bill to spend two nights a week with Rachel. Throughout this process, Rachel was willing to be very flexible, as she understood that securing Susan's cooperation was essential to making this relationship work. And for Susan, what worked was an incremental approach of exposing herself to exactly the situations she feared, and gradually learning to tolerate and even embrace this new situation.

Jim and Joan are a married couple. Joan is bisexual and became involved with Ruth, a lesbian. Because Joan had never been involved with a woman before, Ruth feared that Joan would drop her and go back to her heterosexual life. Ruth demanded more time with Joan, but Jim got very jealous. Faced with two jealous lovers, Joan eventually negotiated an agreement: Jean would spend a few nights a week with Ruth, but each night she would call home to check in with Jim, and would go home if he was feeling too lonely and jealous. Jim agreed that if this worked out, after six months Ruth could move into their home, but this was on Jim's "causes severe jealousy" list. After six months, Jim was not ready to welcome Ruth into the household. He asked to extend for another three months, and by then his jealousy had subsided enough for her to move in.

Some parting words on the engineering model and the phobia model

Most people use a combination of the engineering model and phobia model in their relationships, but lean towards one or the other during a given time period. Both models work well in managing the logistics of relationships, the nuts and bolts of negotiating things like how much time to spend with other partners and what activities are acceptable. It is always easier to legislate those issues that are based on behaviors, so either model can work.

However, behaviors are much easier to control than feelings. You and your partner can much more reliably promise to behave in a certain way, but no one can promise how they are going to feel about a person or a relationship. So the phobia model is usually a much more useful approach to matters such as "I can handle my partner having casual sex but I am frightened of them falling in love with someone else." You can make an agreement that your intention is to stick with casual or secondary outside relationships.

However, you or your partner may develop deeper feelings for someone else, or another relationship may naturally evolve into something more serious over time. If this happens, you have two choices:

1. end that relationship because it does not conform to your engineered agreement, or

2. use the phobia model to incrementally expand that relationship, in the hopes that you can both become comfortable with having more intimate outside relationships over time.

Either path is challenging. If someone asks their partner to end a valued relationship in order to feel safer and to reinforce the primacy of their relationship, it may restore the equilibrium and reassure the primary partner that they are loved. However, sacrificing a relationship with someone they care deeply about may cause intense grieving, as well as anger and resentment towards the primary partner for forcing this choice. The couple may instead use the phobia model to allow the other relationship to expand gradually, to include more time, commitment, and status than was previously agreed upon. This process may be extremely painful for the primary partner to accept, and they may feel betrayed and victimized. I often hear "They promised this would never happen!" while their partner says, "I never intended to fall in love, but it evolved naturally, and I don't want to end it." The process requires trusting your partner and your relationship so completely, and being so invested in your partner's happiness, that you are willing to take the risk of making a radical change in your relationship agreement to accommodate this new reality.

Each relationship situation is unique and there is no "one size fits all" answer. Couples counseling may help craft the best solution for a couple facing this complicated crisis.

Chapter Eleven:

Unlearning the core beliefs that generate jealousy

All our emotional responses and behaviors are reactions which are based on our beliefs. For instance, we wash our hands because we believe in the germ theory, that germs on our hands can spread disease. People who believe in a particular god pray to that god because they believe there is a cause and effect relationship between praying and having those prayers answered, and they behave in ways that their religion teaches them will lead to happiness in an afterlife or heaven.

More emotional examples are that if we believe we will only be loved if we are perfect, we will be devastated by any criticism from a partner. If we believe that being on time shows love and indicates that someone finds us important, then we will feel personally disrespected and unloved if our partner shows up late.

Similarly, certain beliefs generate jealousy, and automatically cause jealous reactions. These beliefs are guaranteed to create jealousy even in the most well-adjusted people. If you want to experience less jealousy, it is necessary to dismantle these three core beliefs.

How much do you believe each of these three core beliefs?

Examine each of the three statements in the following exercise. Ask yourself: In your heart of hearts, how much of you believes each of them? Write each number down on a piece of paper. Is it 90% of yourself that believes them? 50%? Notice which belief is most entrenched, and which one seems least intense for you.

Exercise Sixteen: Core Belief #1

"If my partner really loved me, they wouldn't have any desire for a sexual relationship with anyone else."

This belief sees any interest your partner has in anyone else as a direct reflection of how much they love you. It correlates the *amount* and depth of love to the ability to be interested in having another partner. Its inevitable outcome is that any time your partner shows interest in another person, you will feel intensely jealous because you are convinced that this means your partner does not love you. In this construct, love for you and interest in another partner cannot co-exist: one cancels out the other. It might mean that you will always be struggling to "win" your partner's love or to make them love you "more," believing that if you could only secure their love, they would never be interested in anyone else. If you believe this, you will never be comfortable with your partner having a relationship with anyone else – so before you can succeed in an open relationship, you'll have to find a way to reduce the power of this belief.

Step One: Ask yourself how strong this belief is for you

Do you believe this 100%, or in some lesser amount? Does any part of you believe it might be possible for your partner to love you with all their heart, and still be attracted to someone else? What kinds of things does your partner do to demonstrate their love for you? Do they show their love for you frequently, in numerous ways? Think about a time when your partner has been interested in someone else or has been involved with another lover, either now or in the past. Did you believe that your partner loved you less during this time period? Did it seem like they were taking some of the love that you felt belonged to you and giving that to someone else? Did that make you feel demeaned or less special? Write down your answers to these questions under "Core Belief #1." These questions can be useful in helping you identify the specific beliefs that are creating jealousy for you. Understanding the cause-and-effect relationship between beliefs and jealousy reactions can help you modify your beliefs.

Step Two: Has this belief changed during your relationship?

Next, think back to when you and your partner first developed an open relationship, whether that was at the beginning of the relationship or later on. Ask yourself to what degree you believed this first core belief at the time your relationship first became explicitly polyamorous. If the percentage you believed this was higher at that time than it is now, congratulations! This means that you have made progress since then on reducing the power of this belief. Perhaps you believed it 90% in the beginning and now believe it about 60%. If so, you have made great strides in trusting that your partner has the capacity to love and desire you and still have some romantic interest in another partner, without taking anything away from you. Good job!

The Jealousy Workbook

Step Three: Is this about the past or about your current relationship?

If this belief is particularly strong for you, and it has not changed much, then issues of insecurity and of feeling unloved may predate your current relationship. Perhaps as a child, you always felt your parents loved your siblings more, or a parent was withdrawn or unavailable. Or you may have been neglected in a previous relationship, or had a former lover leave you for someone else. Your life experience may make you hypervigilant for any signs of waning interest by your partner, and you may even imagine these indicators when none exist. You may benefit from exploring your fears and your relationship needs, through individual counseling or some other avenue of personal growth. Strengthening your belief in yourself, and increasing your confidence in creating sufficient love in your life, will go a long way in changing core belief #1, and allowing you to experience less jealousy.

Step Four: Try on a new core belief

You may find this process easier if you consciously try to displace the old belief by inserting a new core belief in its place. Try to substitute the following statement for Core Belief #1:

New Core Belief #1: "My partner loves me so much that they trust our relationship to expand and be enriched by experiencing even more love from others."

When you say this belief out loud to yourself, how does it feel? If it seems ridiculous, this probably means that the first core belief is quite entrenched in your belief system. Examine what you believe about love, romance and relationships, and where those beliefs came from. What kind of role models did you have in childhood of romantic relationships, through your parents' relationship and other relationships you observed? How did these models of love influence your beliefs of what a relationship is supposed to be? What religious teachings might you have experienced about love, sex, marriage, and monogamy? Think about all the movies where th perfect lover solves all of life's problems, all the novels about living happily ever after with that one true love and never needing anyone else, and the pop songs about "only having eyes for you." These influences play a part in instilling a belief that love should include sexual and romantic exclusivity, and that any interest in someone else shows a lack of true love.

Conversely, if you see some kernel of truth in this new core belief #1, this means you have made progress in displacing the initial belief. Take it a little further by thinking about the ways that an outside sexual relationship may help to enhance your primary relationship, such as making your partner more appreciative of you and all your wonderful qualities, creating more romantic "spark" between you and your partner, your partner having more love and attention to give you because they feel recharged and overflowing with love, and creating deeper intimacy between you and your partner due to talking through some of these issues honestly.

Exercise Seventeen: Core Belief #2

"If my partner were happy with me, and if I were a good partner/spouse/lover, my partner would be so satisfied that they wouldn't want to get involved with anyone else."

With the first belief, you were blaming your partner for not loving you enough. <u>This</u> second belief says that if your partner is interested in someone else, it's <u>your</u> fault, for not being the perfect partner. Even worse, you feel like a failure as a person, because your partner's attraction to someone else "proves" you to be lacking in some way. One of my clients called this "my Barbie bridal fantasy" – that her husband "would never even look at another woman because I was supposed to be giving him everything he could ever need."

Step One: Ask yourself how strong this belief is for you

Do you believe this 100%, or in some lesser amount? If this belief is very strong for you, you may need help enhancing your self-esteem, since you have some doubts about your worthiness. You may feel that you do not deserve love or that you are not attractive. Any interest your partner shows in someone else undermines your security about the relationship, as you believe your partner will find someone "better" and will abandon you, confirming your own belief in your inadequacy.

Step Two: Where does this belief come from?

Your doubts about your value may be linked to childhood experiences or painful past romantic relationships. Did you feel rejected by a parent? Were you constantly compared unfavorably with a sibling or criticized for not being "good enough?" Was a parent's approval and acceptance conditional, based on your academic performance, your appearance, or your compliance with your family's demands? We you punished for having opinions of your own, or for rebelling against rigid rules? If so, you may be too invested in winning your partner's approval and terrified of being judged. Your partner's attraction to someone else may feel much more threatening than it really is, as you may feel that they will withdraw their love from you and direct it towards their new love interest. You may be re-playing a childhood drama of struggling for your parents' approval, or trying to allay fears of being unworthy by forcing your partner to prove their loyalty to you through romantic exclusivity. You may find it helpful to write down these childhood experiences and how they may have influenced your beliefs about your value.

Or, you may have had a very painful past relationship where you did not feel loved, where your partner either was indifferent or was not very demonstrative about their feelings for you. Or you may have had a partner who was emotionally unavailable, and you had to struggle to get their attention. You may feel triggered by your current partner having an outside relationship, reactivating the fear of being neglected.

While these insecurities are often caused by painful past experiences, it is also possible that you are suffering from depression or anxiety. Feeling inadequate, worthless, and unlovable are cardinal symptoms of both depression and anxiety. If you believe your low self-esteem may be caused by either of these conditions, it is important to see your health care practitioner for a medical evaluation and treatment.

Step Three: The higher your self-esteem, the less jealousy you will experience

The best strategy for changing this belief is working on enhancing your self-esteem. This is not simple or easy, and won't happen overnight, but is well worth the effort. There are whole books devoted to improving self-esteem, and many workshops and other "self-help" programs for increasing self-confidence and internal security. It is beyond the scope of this book to go into any depth on this complex subject. However, if core belief #2 is strongly entrenched in your belief system, you are likely to benefit from any program designed to enhance self-esteem, including individual counseling, group therapy, self-help books, and workshops. The more confident you feel that you are a desirable partner with something valuable to give in a relationship, the less jealous you will be.

Learning to love yourself and recognize your good qualities is essential for any romantic relationship, because if you don't love yourself, you will never believe that anyone else could really love you either. While this is true in a monogamous relationship, good self-esteem is even more central to the success of a polyamorous relationship. In an open relationship, you are deliberately exposing yourself to challenges to your self-esteem by repeatedly allowing your partner to have sexual relationships with other people. Even the most confident people with great self-esteem may find this bruising to their egos and threatening to their self-image, and people who doubt their own worth can find it devastating. The more you can do to build up your confidence in yourself, the more resilient you will be.

To see whether you have been able to modify Core Belief #2, try on this new belief by saying it out loud to yourself:

Step Four: Try on a new core belief

"My relationship is so solid and trusting that we can experience other relationships freely. My partner is so satisfied with me and our relationship that having other partners will not threaten the bond we enjoy."

What does it feel like to imagine that this new belief could be true for you? If it seems preposterous or unrealistic, then think about why you feel such doubt that your partner is satisfied with you, and what it is that feels so threatening to your relationship. Is there some area of your relationship that feels vulnerable, perhaps an issue that has caused conflict in the past or an aspect of your relationship that has always been problematic? For instance, have you and your partner always had differences in libido? Have sexual differences created conflict in your relationship? Or has your partner frequently asked you to be more supportive, and you have felt criticized for not giving your partner enough focused attention? Have you felt that your partner is disappointed in your way of handling finances? No two people are perfectly compatible, and these areas of conflict may make you feel that your partner will find someone else much more attractive in those arenas that may not be totally satisfying in your relationship.

However, disagreements are normal in any relationship. There is usually no reason to think your partner will leave you or prefer the other partner just because there are some areas where you may be imperfect or where you and your partner have differences.

Having another partner is not an attempt to replace the current partner, but rather to supplement the existing relationship or to add variety. It may be useful to talk with your partner about your fears and clarify whether your partner is in fact dissatisfied with you, or whether they are simply enjoying having an additional relationship. Many people feel reassured by their partner's willingness to disclose their motivation for choosing this particular person for an outside relationship, and to share what it is they are receiving in this other relationship. You probably fear being found inadequate and being replaced, when usually your partner simply wants someone else in addition to you rather than instead of you. Repeating New Core belief #2 out loud to yourself may help you really grasp that key difference, and help you feel secure that outside partners will not threaten the stability or survival of your relationship.

Exercise Eighteen: Core Belief #3

"It's just not possible to love more than one person at the same time."

This belief is built on the "scarcity economy of love," the belief that love is a finite resource and there is only so much to go around. Because most people already feel there are some areas in their relationship where they are not getting enough of something (time, love, affection, sex, support, commitment) they are fearful that they will receive even less if their partner gets involved with additional partners. Embedded in this core belief is the fear that an outside partner will take up so much space in your partner's heart, mind, and schedule that you will be crowded out and that any feelings they have for you will be replaced by their feelings for someone else.

Step One: How much do your believe this?

This belief is based on fears of scarcity and deprivation. Do you believe it with all your heart, or are you less invested in this belief? What percentage of you believes this? If it's more than 50%, this may mean that you have a more generalized fear of deprivation and scarcity in your life, perhaps based on your life experience of always feeling that you were not getting enough from your family during childhood, or in past romantic relationships with people who were not available to meet your needs. And many people who have suffered deprivation of any resource often generalize that experience into an intense fear of scarcity in all arenas.

For instance, people who were raised in poverty, where they could not count on adequate food, shelter, and medical care, may find that romantic jealousy triggers their fears of never getting enough of the necessities in life, including love. Years of struggling for scarce resources can create the belief that they will always be competing for crumbs. Or, this core belief may be based in your current relationship, feeling your partner never gives you enough time, affection, sex, or emotional intimacy. If you are already feeling that your core needs are not being met, you may be triggered by an open relationship to believe you will be starved for love.

Step Two: Is it more about the perceived quality than the quantity of love?

For many people, this core belief has less to do with scarcity than a fear that an outside relationship will "cheapen" the love their partner has for them, destroying the specialness of the bond between them. Some people are convinced that an outside relationship will change the status of their primary relationship, demoting them from the love of their partner's life to just one of many interchangeable people. This belief seems more common in women, who have been socialized to associate sex with intimacy and a deep connection with their partner. It is often nearly impossible for them to imagine that their partner could have sex and intimacy with someone else without diluting their pair bond in some negative way. On some level they believe that "my partner can only have that with me." They may experience this change as a very painful loss of their unique status in their partner's life, feeling that they are becoming less loved and less important. They need reassurance that this new relationship will not displace or replace them, and that their partner still loves them just as much as before the new relationship came into the picture. It helps if their partner reminds them frequently about how and why they are still special, and the reasons they remain committed to the relationship.

The good news is that many people find this core belief easier to challenge than the other two! Many people have had the experience of deeply loving more than one person at a time. For instance, many couples report that when they have a child, they love the child as much as their spouse, but adding that new relationship does not reduce their love for their spouse. And parents who have more than one child love the second child as much as the first, and have room in their hearts to cherish both children without one receiving less love.

Perhaps you remember having a wonderful best friend in junior high school and then developing an additional very close friendship with a new person, but not being any less attached to the initial best friend. So it is not such a stretch to imagine that you could have a romantic relationship with a new person without displacing the love you feel for your spouse. Even many people in monogamous relationships admit that they have had intense crushes or even fallen in love with someone else while still loving their spouse, but never acted on those feelings. Since so many people have had first-hand experience which contradicts this core belief that you cannot love more than one person, they can believe that their partner could have an outside relationship without loving them any less.

Step Three: Try on a new core belief

New Core Belief #3: "There is an abundance of love in the world and there is plenty for everyone. Loving more than one person is a choice that can exponentially expand my potential for giving and receiving love."

How does it feel to you to say this new core belief out loud? Does it feel true or not? Ask yourself if there was ever a time, in the past or the present, when you loved more than one person, whether romantically or in other ways. Try to remember precisely when you realized that you loved the new person, in addition to loving the existing friend/lover/child/parent/sibling. How did that feel, to be full of love for more than one person at the same time? Notice the difference in the exact type of love you feel for each person – for instance, the familial love for a sibling, the parental love for a new baby, the abiding loyalty you feel towards a close friend, the passionate love for a new "crush," or the deep love you feel for your spouse. You may love each person equally in terms of "how much" you love them, but you may notice that there are differences in "how" you love them, and what that love is about. The kind of love you feel for your mother is different than the kind of love you feel for your spouse, but you probably do not feel that you love one or the other of them "more." It may be difficult to objectively evaluate the feelings you have for each of them, as you are comparing "apples and oranges."

When you are in a long-term relationship, you have a strong commitment, deep love, trust, companionship, predictability, and the experience of being truly seen, loved, and accepted for who you are. When you have a budding new love affair, you experience the excitement of sexual fantasy, the mystery of someone new and different, the potential for personal growth, as well as the thrill of taking risks. So the love you feel for this new person may be an infatuation, based on your projection that they are going to be the perfect lover, rather than being grounded in who they really are. You know your long-term partner too well to sustain the fantasy that they are perfect and will meet all your needs, as reality has already proved otherwise. So the two types of love are very different and may be difficult to see clearly, especially because New Relationship Energy can be so intense.

In recalling this situation or others like it, you may be able to confirm that you are capable of loving more than one person simultaneously, and that realization can help to experience new core belief #3 and reduce your jealousy when your partner has an outside sexual relationship.

Parting words on the Three Core Beliefs

Because each of these beliefs is connected to a very primal fear, they take time and effort to dislodge from your belief system. The first belief expresses a deep fear that you are not loved and will be abandoned. The second taps into our insecurities and the fear that we are not adequate or deserving of love. The third is a fear of deprivation and being starved for love and attention, or being demoted from the one and only to a lesser status in our partner's life. Be patient with yourself and your partner in trying to dissect these beliefs, gradually replacing them with new core beliefs that will support your polyamorous lifestyle and help you let go of jealous reactions. For most of us, this is an ongoing process that will take place gradually with years of practice and experience.

Chapter Twelve:

What if your partner is jealous?

Most of this book is designed to help you when you are experiencing a jealousy attack. However, if you are in an open relationship, it is very likely that your partner will also experience jealousy. Many people find this experience even more painful and scary than managing their own jealousy.

It can be a shock to see your partner suffering with intensely jealous reactions, and possibly lashing out at you. You may feel hurt and confused because you may not have done anything "wrong" or outside your relationship agreement, yet your partner is angry and losing control of their composure and perhaps their behaviors. What can you do to help your partner feel better and reduce the conflict?

Exercise Nineteen: Technique for helping a jealous partner

Step One: Your mantra: shut up and listen!

First and foremost, when faced with a jealous partner, your mantra should be to tell yourself over and over, internally: "Just shut up and listen!"

When your partner expresses jealous feelings, the most effective response is empathy and good communication. Listen carefully to your partner's words, as well as their non-verbal communication and body language. Let them talk, without interruptions, until they seem to have completed what they are trying to say. You will probably find this very difficult because they may be making untrue accusations or exaggerating the situation, since their pain may create distorted perceptions about this situation. You will probably feel very defensive and want to "fight back" by making an impressive argument for your side. Remember – this is not a courtroom, where you are trying to convince a jury of your innocence; it is your relationship, and your partner is experiencing a lot of pain and trying to express it. Be patient and try not to argue. It is imperative that you avoid being reactive, and instead seek information from them and acknowledge what they are feeling.

Step Two: Ask for more information and clarification of feelings

Ask your partner if they are feeling fear, sadness, and/or anger, and roughly the ratio of those three primary emotions (you may want to refer to the "Jealousy Pie chart" exercise in this book). See if they can describe exactly what the feelings are, and the source of these feelings. Acknowledge that you have heard and understood what your partner is experiencing. Even if you do not agree, you can understand that they are in pain and can see how they got there. Giving your partner that validation can go a long way to helping to reduce the jealousy and repair the intimacy that has been disrupted by this incident.

Step Three: Allow them to have their feelings!

Don't try to "fix it" for them by trying to make those feelings go away or challenging the rational basis for those feelings. Allow them to have their feelings, don't invalidate their experience! They probably already feel embarrassed to be having these feelings and may already have been beating themselves up for feeling this way, so they will be crushed if you dismiss their pain and tell them how they "should" feel. It can be helpful for you to paraphrase some of what they have said and repeat that back to them, so they know you heard and understood them, and they can correct or clarify if you have gotten part of it wrong.

Step Four: Identify your role in the problem

See if you or your partner can identify what part you played in triggering the jealous response, and take responsibility for any of your own behaviors or attitudes that you would consider modifying. You are bound to feel defensive, and your natural response will be to justify your behavior. Instead, apologize for any actual mistakes you have made, even if your partner's response seems out of proportion to the situation.

Step Five: Ask for the floor, to tell your side of the story and express your feelings

After your partner feels safe and is less reactive, ask if they are willing to listen to your feelings about what happened. It is important to get their consent before launching into telling your side of the story, as they may be feeling too wounded right now to hear your experience. You have a right to be heard and to address any distortions or misunderstandings of your behavior and motives. However, this may not be the ideal time, and you may have to agree to talk about your feelings later when your partner is calmer and more emotionally resilient. If your partner says they can't handle that right now, don't push it, because no good will come of it. You will only go down a path of accusations and recriminations, and will sabotage any chance of resolving this issue.

If your partner feels ready to hear your experience, try to calmly explain what happened, why you behaved as you did, what you believe your agreement is with your partner, and your feelings and thoughts about it. If you feel that your partner has distorted your motives or exaggerated your transgressions, try to express that in as neutral a way as possible, and ask if they would be willing to restate things in a way you believe is more accurate. Rather than criticizing your partner, tell them how it hurts you when they say things about you that you feel are not fair. Try to remain open and focus on how you actually feel, right now.

Step Six: Think carefully before making any new agreements.

Don't rush into making any commitment about what to do differently in the future. Don't agree to something just to appease your partner if you are going to resent it later. Can you actually deliver on your agreements? Will you find this new agreement too restrictive and be tempted to break it or to demand a change later? If you commit to something just because you are so distressed by your partner's pain or anger, you will just create more distrust and jealousy in the future.

Example:

Tom went on a date with a new woman. His partner Rachel had asked that he not go farther than making out on the first date, and to come home by 11:00 PM so they could get a good night's sleep. He went to his new flame's house for dinner, and they cuddled on the couch for a couple of hours. When he came home at 11:30 PM, Rachel was irate about him being late, and began shouting at him that he had lied to her and that she couldn't trust him. He wanted to yell back that being thirty minutes late was no big deal and that she was overreacting and had no right to be angry at him. Instead, he took a deep breath and apologized for being late, saying that he did not realize it would upset her (Step One: Shut up and listen!). She immediately felt relieved that he was being supportive and taking responsibility for being late. She then confided that she knew it was irrational, but that when he didn't come home right at 11:00, she became terrified that he was not going to come home at all. He asked her if she was upset about his making out with his new date, or whether it was his being late that caused her jealousy (Step Two: Ask for more information and clarification). She said, "It's hard enough for me to be sitting here at home, knowing you are with another woman, but when you are late I become really freaked out." (Step Three: Allow your partner to have their feelings). He told her he understood that him going on a date was stressful for her, and that his being late made it worse for her. (Step Four: Identify your role in the problem). He had created a safe space for her by accepting her feelings, and was able to mirror them back to her. As a result, they both felt a little better right away, rather than escalating into a fight.

So Rachel and Tom successfully negotiated Steps One through Four. Great job!

Then he initiated Step Five, by asking her if she would be open to hearing how this situation felt to him. She said she felt too upset, but suggested two possible options for Tom to explain his side:

1) that they talk about it the next morning after having some sleep, or 2) that if it felt urgent to him to express himself right away, that he write her an email before going to bed, and she promised to read it in the morning and talk with him about it then. He said he could wait until morning to discuss it, but that he appreciated the email option. Then she asked him to commit to being home on time in the future. In keeping with Step Six, he hesitated and said that he was reluctant to agree to this, because the reason he was late was that he and his new partner were cuddling and talking and he did not want to "destroy the mood" by looking for a clock to see what time it was, and rushing out the door when they were feeling close. He asked for flexibility for future dates, such as allowing him to be as much as an hour late, or not to make a specific time for him to come home. He asked if he could just come home in the morning, but Rachel said she wasn't ready for that yet and wanted to try a few more dates where he came home by 11:00 or 12:00. They made an agreement that he would try to get home by 11:00 PM, but that as long as he was home by midnight, she would accept that.

Parting words on coping with your partner's jealousy

Jealousy is all about feelings, and an argument is all about intellectual analysis. Be a lover, not a lawyer!

When your partner is in the midst of a jealousy attack, they need compassion and reassurance that they are loved. Often, their jealousy triggers a defensive response and a huge argument. When this happens, you and your partner are working at cross-purposes and not actually communicating. You are trying to reconnect and experience a loving bond. If you find yourself going down this path of argument, buttressing your case with intellectual reasoning, ask for a brief time-out. Then start over by trying to be present, hear your partner's feelings, and make your best effort to understand their experience and give them love and acceptance.

Your other mantra: Remind your partner that you love them!

During any jealousy episode, remind your partner how much you love them and how precious the relationship is to you. Assure them that you will not do anything to jeopardize the stability of your relationship, and that you are working together as a team to set healthy boundaries that will strengthen your connection with your partner. As much as possible, you are trying to be allies and solve this problem through cooperation, rather than falling into an antagonistic stance and trying to "win." You may win the battle through perfect debating in circles around your partner's feelings, but will lose the war by destroying your relationship.

Chapter Thirteen:

The three circles of "Poly Hell": Common jealousy triggers, and strategies for managing them

Many people who are in a primary relationship stumble into an outside relationship either by choice or by chance, and, once involved, find that things have gone terribly awry.

Three key behaviors can put you into what I call "Poly Hell" – an intolerable situation where things feel out of control and your primary relationship feels like it is being destroyed by an outside relationship. The techniques in this section offer some strategies for either mitigating these problems by proactively avoiding them, or for effectively addressing them when they do arise.

The most typical poly dilemmas are inevitably created when the partner with the outside relationship devotes too much time and energy to the new relationship and ignores or neglects the partner at home.

This phenomenon is to some degree understandable – since a new romance, even if casual or "secondary," is often imbued with the infamous "New Relationship Energy," or NRE. NRE involves a lot of fantasy and projection. When we first get involved with someone, we imagine them to be the perfect person and

ideal romantic partner we have been longing for, since we don't know them very well yet and do not know all their bad habits and annoying behaviors. That's an unbeatable combination of novelty, mystery, and chemistry, mixed with our own romantic fantasies. And our new partner is on their best behavior and trying to impress us by exhibiting their most attractive qualities. So there is some excuse for getting distracted by the "shiny new toy" aspect of a hot new love affair, wanting to spend a lot of time exploring this new person and thinking about them obsessively.

On the other hand, it is also understandable that the partner who is left at home will feel extremely threatened by this new relationship that seems to be taking over your life. So some compromise must be struck between the compelling desire to bask in this fun and exciting new experience, and the pre-existing partner's need for reassurance and attention.

The three circles of Poly Hell

The most common problems growing out of this tension between competing needs are what I call demotion, displacement, and intrusion.

Demotion:
the first circle of poly hell

The primary partner has previously had you all to him-or herself, and has not had to share your time, affection, attention, and loyalty with another lover. Most partners take this hegemony for granted until a new partner enters the picture. Suddenly the primary partner feels demoted from "the one and only" to being one of two partners.

This is a huge shock to anyone who is experiencing it for the first time. We have no training for sharing our lover's romantic attention with someone else, and most people find it disorienting and painful. Some amount of demotion is inevitable, as some portion of the partner's attention will necessarily be diverted from the primary relationship to the new partner. Things are different now that we can no longer depend on having a monopoly on our partner's romantic energy. It doesn't mean our partner loves us less, or that we are less important to them, it just means there is another person who has some small claim on our partner's time and affection.

Exercise Twenty: Ease the adjustment to sharing your partner with clear communication

Step One: Use a speaker symbol to practice supportive listening

The first step is for the partner who feels demoted to express their feelings, and the partner who has a new relationship to listen and acknowledge their partner's feelings and concerns.

At a time when you are not feeling rushed, sit down to talk with your partner and agree to a time limit of an hour. Set a timer for twenty minutes, and the partner who is feeling demoted, who I'll call Partner A, should speak first. I recommend using what I call a "speaker symbol," with Partner A holding onto an object that shows that this person has the floor and is not to be interrupted. This can be a stone, a talking stick, a candle, a bowl, a ring or pendant, or any small object. As long as Partner A is holding the speaker symbol, they may speak for as long as they want, or until the timer rings.

After twenty minutes, see if Partner A wants more time. If so, agree to set the timer for ten more minutes, but no longer. During this initial time, while Partner A has the speaker symbol, Partner B practices "supportive listening." This is much harder than it sounds! Supportive listening means doing everything possible to make your partner feel heard and understood. It includes things like facing your partner, keeping eye contact, nodding your head to show you are getting the message, and maintaining friendly and attentive facial expressions. Supportive listening also requires that partner B speaks only to support their partner fully expressing him or herself. This means only saying things like "Thank you for sharing that," "I think I understand what you mean," "I can see that must have been painful for you," "I'm not sure I quite understand. Could you say more to help me understand better?"

During this initial transition, Partner A often reports experiencing sadness, betrayal, distrust, a sense of loss and grieving, fears of abandonment. Partner B will often makes the situation worse if they ignore the speaker symbol – by denying that there is any loss, ridiculing or dismissing their partner's fears, and stressing that this new relationship will actually enhance the primary relationship. While such talk is sincere and is intended to reassure the partner that they have nothing to fear and that the primary relationship is not in jeopardy, it is bound to backfire by making the partner feel invalidated. Instead, Partner B should try to acknowledge that A has lost something: they have lost the primacy of being the one and only lover, and they need to grieve that loss, even though in the long run the new relationship may have an overall positive effect on the primary relationship which may outweigh that loss. The best approach is to simply listen and provide supportive feedback as needed.

Step Two: Trade roles

Now it is time to trade roles. If you are Partner A, the partner who feels demoted, give the "speaker symbol" to Partner B, and set the timer again for twenty minutes. First, they should spend a few minutes trying to paraphrase what you have just told them, to make sure they have heard and understood why you feel demoted by the new relationship. If they do not have it exactly right, gently ask if you can clarify. Only do so if they agree to stop the timer and give you the speaker symbol, then add a brief clarifying statement. Turn the timer back on and allow them to spend the rest of their twenty minutes saying how they feel about this situation, and how they see the role of the outside relationship in relation to your relationship. While they are talking, use only supportive listening, as described above: use body language to let them know you are getting everything, and speak only to support them to express their feelings and experience. You do not have to agree with what they say, just confirm that you heard them and understand what they are going through, even if your perspective is very different. After the timer goes off, set it for ten more minutes , if desired, and then ask any additional questions you may have about their statements.

Step Three: Use written communication to develop some agreements

It is important that both people articulate their needs and negotiate what the partners can reasonably expect from each other. Each partner should write down on a piece of paper the answers to the following questions:

How much time do each of you feel is appropriate for the partner with the outside relationship to spend with this new person? Are overnights okay or not? What about weekends? Will holidays be reserved for the preexisting relationship, or can some holidays or some part of a holiday be spent with the other partner?

What kind of sexual activities are allowed with the new partner, and what will be off-limits and reserved for the primary relationship? For instance, are some sexual activities reserved for the primary relationship, or is blanket permission granted for any and all sexual activities?

What about social activities? Will the new partner be included in special occasions, parties and other social events along with the primary partner, or will each relationship be kept separate?

Will the new relationship be kept private and discreet, or will friends, family, and work associates be told about the new person?

Step Four: Compare notes

1. Compare what you have written down with your partner's answers to the questions in Step Two. How much overlap is there?

The Jealousy Workbook

2. Underline in black ink any areas where you both agree, and confirm that you both mean the same thing by the words you have used, then write those guidelines on a separate piece of paper. Give yourselves some credit and congratulations for the fact that you have agreement on a number of important issues! Thank each other for being loving and communicating clearly.

3. Circle or underline in red ink any areas where there is disagreement, conflict, or confusion. Look for a few of these areas where there may be room for compromise, or where you may not be so far apart. See if you can each stretch to agree on a few of these items. Another strategy is to "trade:": pick a few issues that are not "bottom-line" issues for you and agree to drop one if your partner will also drop one issue that they do not feel is non-negotiable. Sometimes this strategy can create enough good will and trust that it becomes easier to tackle the larger issues. If there are some things you are not sure about or are a little reluctant to agree to, consider saying, "Let's try that for a month and see how it works, with the caveat that if I am not comfortable with it after a month, we'll drop it." You may want to add a section to your written agreement that are "provisional" items, which you are willing to try for some period of time but are not being added to the long-term agreement at this time.

Because "demotion" is about feeling knocked off the pedestal of being the one and only lover, this exercise focuses on identifying what will be kept special and exclusive to the preexisting relationship and what will be allowed in the new relationship. What kind of boundaries will bracket that relationship? The partner who has initiated an outside relationship can reduce their partner's anxiety and jealousy through frequent reassurances of their loyalty and by consistently keeping agreements in order to foster greater trust.

Step Five: Look into your past

If you find yourself having such an intense reaction that is seems out of proportion, these feelings are probably generated by something from your past, not the present situation of demotion. Try to rate your reaction on a scale of zero to ten, then ask yourself what number would really be reasonable for the current situation. For instance, if your feelings are an 8, and you rate the appropriate response as a 4, there may be some past trauma that is being triggered or old wounds re-opened. Try to remember a time in your past when you felt this same way, usually in childhood but sometimes in an adult relationship where you have felt betrayed or abandoned. Counseling or a support group may help you discover the origin of these feelings and learn to separate past trauma from the present poly situation. Remember that you are no longer a child trapped in a traumatic situation; you are an adult who can take care of yourself and ask for what you need to feel safe.

Two examples:

Jesse thought he would be fine with his wife having outside partners. However, when she did become romantically involved with another man, he had panic attacks and episodes of rage. He rated his feelings a 10, but guessed that a "reasonable person" would respond at an intensisty of a 2 or 3. He realized that this situation was very reminiscent of his childhood, as he was an only child until he was ten years old, when his baby brother was born. He experienced intense sibling rivalry, as he felt betrayed by his parents for demoting him from the only child to being one of two sons. With the birth of a sibling, things will never be the same again, as the children will always have to share their parents' love, loyalty, time, and attention. This entails loss and grief, even if eventually the joy of having a sibling outweighs the loss of the parents' total devotion. With an open relationship, it is inevitable that there will be some loss and grief when someone who had a monopoly on their partner's romantic attention has to share that status with another lover.

Another example:

Laverne experienced intense episodes of jealousy and felt completely betrayed when her female primary partner became involved with another woman. She rated her feelings a 9, but felt the situation warranted about a 6. She had been raised by a very devoted single mother, who married a new man when Laverne was eight years old. She was devastated that her mother's love and attention was now being partially diverted to the husband. The poly situation was bringing back those same feelings of shock, betrayal and exclusion. Counseling helped her see that she was being triggered by her childhood pain and she was able to work through these feelings rather than blaming her partner's new relationship.

Displacement:
the second circle of poly hell

Displacement is a feeling that a partner's outside relationship is receiving so much time, attention, and loyalty that it is crowding out the primary relationship. The partner at home feels abandoned and disrespected, and suspects that they are being replaced by the new person. Their partner spends too much time seeing the new partner, calling, texting, or emailing them.

What's the difference between demotion and displacement? Some people have expressed confusion on this point. Demotion is about the change in status of the primary relationship, as the partner no longer has an exclusive relationship. Displacement is more about the loss of time and attention. So demotion is about loss of exclusive rights and roles, while displacement is more about logistics and the practical reality of time and energy.

Exercise Twenty-one: Tips to minimize displacement

Some feelings of displacement are inevitable, because having a new relationship almost always takes some time and energy away from the primary relationship. However, a few important steps can minimize the problem.

If you are the partner with an outside relationship

1. Be diligent in providing adequate time and attention to your primary partner as well as the new partner. Spending quality time together can often compensate for spending slightly less time together. Romantic activities with your primary partner, and having special dates like you used to when you first got together, can reduce feelings of displacement. Make your partner feel special and important, rather than cast aside for the "shiny new toy."

2. Give your primary partner affection and gestures of romantic attention. Most people are reassured by a brief "love note" or card on their pillow, being surprised with a favorite home-cooked meal, or a phone call just to say you miss them. Don't neglect some of the nice gestures that can nurture your primary relationship and assure your partner of your love.

3. Be transparent about the outside relationship. Every relationship deserves some privacy, and you don't have to share every detail. But being too secretive will make your primary partner feel even more left out and create unnecessary suspicion. So try to negotiate an agreement that gives them enough disclosure to feel included in this important part of your life. This is especially important if you are the kind of couple that has always talked about everything going on in your lives.

4. Consider some joint activities that the three of you can do together. If both your partners are comfortable with it, consider including your primary partner in occasional social activities with the other partner. Getting together for lunch, a bike ride, or going to a party together may help your primary partner to feel included in this part of your life.

A few examples:

Jack and his new partner Jennifer enjoyed going to art galleries and museums. Jennifer encouraged Jack to invite his wife Leah to a monthly art event she attended. Leah realized she felt envious of Jack and Jennifer going to all these shows, hobnobbing with artists and drinking wine. The three of them started going together each month to this event; it became a bonding experience that helped Leah feel included in Jack's other relationship as well as feeling part of his involvement in the arts community.

Juan and Russell lived together for twelve years, and had always enjoyed three-way sexual experiences together with other men they met at local bars and clubs. However, Juan developed an ongoing relationship with

The Jealousy Workbook

Joaquin, and Russell felt left out when they had private dates and he was alone at home. He became jealous that Juan was bringing Joaquin flowers, and frequently texting him with graphic sexual suggestions. Russell's feelings of displacement were relieved when Juan took him away on a vacation to Belize, where they had gone on their honeymoon eight years before. They lounged on the beaches, enjoyed candlelight dinners, went out to clubs together, and rekindled their romance.

Intrusion: the third circle of poly hell

Intrusion refers to the way an outside relationship has the tendency to invade the time and space of the primary relationship and make the primary partner feel unsafe.

When we are spending time with our primary partner, we may feel the need or desire to stay in close contact with the outside partner. We may spend a little time, or a lot of time, phoning, texting, or chatting with them online, when we are "supposed" to be giving attention to the primary partner. This can be especially difficult at the beginning of a new relationship, when infatuation is intense. The primary partner's anxieties are likely to be higher at the beginning of a new relationship if the other relationship invades their time and space.

It is even more painful if, in fact, we are gradually beginning to spend more and more time with the new partner, triggering a fear of being abandoned and replaced by this new partner. Often the person having the new relationship is under the influence of lust and infatuation, and feels so motivated to pursue this exciting new love affair that they ignore their primary partner's pleas for time and attention. They rationalize that they must focus on the new partner to solidify that relationship or it may not survive. At the same time, they see the primary relationship as stable and secure. As a result, they take their relationship for granted and fail to grasp that it needs maintenance and sustenance in order to thrive.

The damage done by neglect during this phase can often be fatal to the primary relationship, especially if the primary partner is experiencing a scarcity of time and romance with their partner, and their pleas for their partner to focus attention on the relationship fall on deaf ears. As one such man said, "Not only was she spending most of her time with this other guy, but whenever I tried to tell her how I felt, she ignored me and didn't seem to care that I was very unhappy." Eventually, they feel so abandoned and humiliated that they are likely to leave the relationship, because the cumulative affect of unmet needs will necessitate them shifting their own relationship energy elsewhere to another partner (or partners) who will be more attentive and available.

Unfortunately, it is only at the point that the primary partner decides to end the relationship that the partner usually takes their demands seriously, because they have been oblivious and naively believed that the relationship was secure. And by then it is usually too late to repair the damage, as their partner is already on their way out the door, and feels so mistreated and distrustful they are unlikely to be deterred.

Exercise Twenty-two: Tips for managing and reducing intrusion

If you are the partner who is experiencing intrusion due to your partner's other relationship, these ideas may help you:

Step One: Accept that some amount of intrusion is inevitable in any open relationship

It is impossible to compartmentalize relationships so completely that one relationship will never intrude in any way on another relationship. You are likely to have hurt feelings and will need to learn to handle a tolerable amount of disappointment due to these intrusions. For example, one partner may have an acute need, while you are in the middle of a date with the other partner – needing to be driven to the emergency room, or having a "poly meltdown" at a very inconvenient moment.

Expect a few "oops" moments in any poly relationship, such as accidentally scheduling a date with one partner on the other partner's birthday, or agreeing to spend time with one partner when you have already committed to do something else with the other partner.

Try to be forgiving when your partner isn't perfect. People do make mistakes, and you will be crushed if you expect your partner to behave perfectly in all situations. These intrusions can be handled rationally by most partners as long as they don't happen too often and have some valid reason. Keep in mind that you may make similar mistakes yourself in juggling more than one relationship, and will not want to be held to such impossible standards of behavior when the tables are turned.

Remember that these small intrusions will become much easier to handle over time. Some of the charge goes out of the situation after a while, as all partners prove themselves to be reliable and trustworthy, and give each other more slack as time goes on.

Step Two: Give your partners three "Get Out of Jail Free" cards.

Just assume that their will be some intrusions that will cause you pain, as your partner is on a steep learning curve in balancing their own needs and the needs of multiple partners. Each time your partner's other relationships intrudes on your relationship, your partner uses up one of their "Get out of jail free" cards. The goal of these cards is for your partner to try their best to prevent intrusions, and to have a visible way of being accountable when they do happen. By the time they use up all three cards, you may be more tolerant of occasional invasions into your relationship, and your partner will have a much better skill set to prevent them.

A few examples:

Rosa and Anita lived together, and Rosa developed another relationship with Suzanne. Suzanne was single, and frequently became lonely and called Rosa asking for dates when she was with Anita. At first, Anita agreed to give up some of her time in order to accommodate Suzanne's needs. However, she became very resentful when Rosa canceled a special dinner date, celebrating her promotion at work, in order to see Suzanne. Rosa had already used up her third "get out of jail free" card, and promised Anita to set firmer boundaries with Suzanne to stick to the amount of time they had already negotiated.

Scott and his wife Marisa argued because Scott repeatedly double-booked dates with her on the same nights he made plans with his boyfriend Mick. He apologized profusely and reminded Marisa that he had always had difficulties with scheduling. She acknowledged that she was much more upset about poly scheduling snafus than she had been in the past when he scheduled a bowling night on their date night. They agreed to try an online calendar and go over their schedules every week, and these efforts reduced the intrusions.

Step Three: Ask for appropriate boundaries on contact with the other partner: Establish some guidelines about how much, how often, and in what ways the outside relationship may intrude on the primary relationship.

Ask yourself these questions:

- Is it okay if your partner talks to their other partner on the phone while on a date with you? ☐ yes ☐ no

- What about texting their other partner in your presence? ☐ yes ☐ no

- Can they discreetly email the other partner while they are on the computer doing other tasks? ☐ yes ☐ no

- Would it be okay to call, text, or email their other partners while you are in another room doing something else, such as when you are in the shower or putting the kids to bed? ☐ yes ☐ no

- Should they leave the room if they need to call or email their other partner? ☐ yes ☐ no

- If they do contact the other partner while spending time with you, do you want a specific time limit, such as ten minutes, or perhaps a limit on how often, such as once a day? ☐ yes ☐ no

_____minutes for each contact   _____frequency of contact

There is no right or wrong way to do this, as long as everyone is comfortable with the situation and can tolerate the degree of intrusion involved. However, if you answered "no" to all five questions, your expectations are not realistic for a polyamorous relationship. While it is reasonable to expect your partner to give you their undivided attention most of the time when you are together, you must find some way to allow them to stay in touch with their other partners, at least in some minimal way. Think about what would be the least painful way for you to create an opening for contact, such as an occasional discreet text or email, or a short phone call to another partner while you are on the phone or occupied with a household task.

A few examples:

Jean felt insulted and ignored when they were eating at a restaurant and Ron sent a text to his girlfriend Julie. And Julie would often call him when they were at home watching a movie in the evenings. They made an agreement that Julie could call him at work as often as she wanted, and he could text or call her from work, on his lunch hour, or during his commute. He agreed not to have contact with Julie when Jean and Ron were spending time together, unless there was an urgent reason – "urgent" being defined as physical illness, extreme emotional distress, or an immediate change of plans.

Larry was annoyed that his husband Tom spent too much time on the phone with his submissive, Ken. Ken wanted frequent contact with Tom, since their D/s relationship included Tom providing supervision and direction to Ken. They made an agreement that he would call Ken once in the morning for fifteen minutes and once in the evening for fifteen minutes, and could email him during the day if Ken needed more instruction and interaction. This allowed Larry to have Tom's undivided attention for most of their time together, and created a safe container for Ken to feel supported.

Compartmentalization as a survival strategy in open relationships

Some people find that any reminder of their partner's other relationship is excruciatingly painful, and that any intrusion ruins the entire date or even creates distress for the rest of the week. Being exposed to the other relationship in any way makes them feel unloved and disrespected, as if their partner is rejecting them and demonstrating that the other partner is more important or desirable.

Does this sound familiar? This usually means that you have compartmentalized your partner's other relationship as a survival strategy to manage your jealousy. In other words, an open relationship is much more comfortable for some people if they can just focus on being with their partner and to some extent pretend that there is no other partner in the picture. You mentally place your partner's other relationship in a "compartment," as if putting it on a shelf and closing the door. This is not the same as denial, as you know full well that your partner has another partner. It's just easier for you to fully open yourself to being present with your partner if you are able to temporarily forget about that other relationship. This is a very successful strategy for many people to become more comfortable in an open relationship, as they risk shutting down emotionally if they have to have their partner's other relationship "in their face" when they are trying to stay connected.

People who compartmentalize prefer to have very little information about their partners' other relationships. This coping strategy works because the less they think about it, the safer they feel, and life goes on more smoothly and comfortably. It appears to be based on personality and temperament and how people process information. The more they know about a partner's outside relationships, the more anxious they become. Having more information only gives them more distressing facts to focus on, and encourages them to obsess about uncomfortable images of their partner with another lover. When it comes to disclosure, more is not always better, as any information can be an intrusion. Appropriate levels of disclosure will be discussed further in Exercise Thirty on p. 120.

Exercise Twenty-three: Educating your partner about compartmentalization

Step One: Communicate clearly with your partner about your need to compartmentalize

If you need this level of compartmentalization to feel secure and loved, help your partner understand your needs. Explain to your partner that you want them to have as little contact with their other partners as possible while in your company, and that any contact with their other partner should be out of your sight (and hearing) so that you are not aware of it.

Step Two: Privacy is not the same as secrecy

Your partner may be trying to be transparent by contacting their other partners openly, rather than being secretive. It is also possible they are just not aware of the pain they are inadvertently causing. Remind your partner that you need privacy from their other relationship, and that privacy and secrecy are two different things. Explain that this compartmentalization will allow you to be closer to them and fully enjoy the time you spend together, rather than being triggered into a state of sadness, anxiety, and distancing from them.

Exercise Twenty-four: How to manage the more subtle intrusions

Step One: Identify the symptoms of indirect intrusions

An outside relationship can also intrude in less obvious ways. Does your partner do any of the following:

- Are they too tired for sex because they had a date with the other partner and didn't get enough sleep? ☐ yes ☐ no

- Do they seem distant and distracted during a date with you because they are thinking about something going on in the other relationship? ☐ yes ☐ no

- Does your partner talk way too much about their other relationship, allowing this to take over your time together? ☐ yes ☐ no

- Are scheduling conflicts and logistics starting to feel very invasive to your relationship? Does it seem like this other relationship is intruding on special occasions like birthdays, holidays, vacations, and travel plans? ☐ yes ☐ no

Step Two: Identify possible solutions to minimize intrusions

If you answered "yes" to some or all of the above questions, here are some tips for reducing these intrusions.

- Ask your partner to commit to more time together, even if it means taking time away from work or some other activity to give the primary relationship more attention.

- If you are lacking some specific type of attention, ask your partner directly to provide that. Don't expect them to guess that you need more affection, more verbal affirmations of their love, more romantic gestures, or other behaviors that will counteract your resentment about the intrusions caused by their other relationship.

- Go with your partner to a poly support group or social group. This can be very helpful, as you can talk with others about what works for them, and can see healthy models of working out these conflicts. You will also hear cautionary tales from others about relationships that have been destroyed by too much intrusion.

- If you and your partner cannot come to some resolution on your own, couples counseling may help to give both partners a "reality check" on reasonable expectations and standards of behavior.

A few parting words on Poly Hell

Some amount of demotion, displacement, and intrusion are inevitable in any open relationship, and are likely to create some conflict. It will require a lot of negotiation to allow the partner with an outside relationship enough freedom to pursue that relationship, while creating enough safety and comfort for the partner at home. Everyone will need to compromise to achieve the best balance.

If you are the partner experiencing these three very painful symptoms, don't expect yourself to be completely comfortable. For most of us, it is not realistic to be confronted with our partner's other relationships without some hurt feelings and anxiety. Don't make it worse by beating up on yourself or your partner for the friction and distress that will naturally occur. Over time it is likely to get much easier as you become more resilient and feel more secure, and as your partner learns how to avoid triggering your "sore spots."

Chapter Fourteen:

Communication skills for people in open relationships

While excellent communication skills are a prerequisite for any healthy, happy relationship, this is even more true in open relationships. Monogamous couples often can get by on assumptions based on the old model of the traditional heterosexual marriage. People in open relationships cannot count on any or all of our partners having the same rules in mind unless we clearly voice our needs and expectations and make explicit relationship agreements.

Exercise Twenty-five: Basic steps of successful communication

In my experience, these are the most important things to remember in communicating with your partner(s) and resolving polyamorous dilemmas.

Step One: Keep it as simple as possible

Any communication techniques should be simple enough for you and your partners to utilize during a conflict, when emotions are high and no one is at their best. When one or more people are feeling angry, hurt, or frightened, any complicated communication technique is likely to go out the window. To be useful, any technique has to be simple enough to remember and put into action when you or your partner(s) are at your worst.

Step Two: Avoid barriers to effective listening

I see couples every day for counseling who have gotten in a world of trouble because they are not actually listening to each other. This is often most true in long-term relationships, as there is an unfortunate tendency to think we know our partners so well that we no longer have to listen to them.

Pay attention to your partner's body language, tone of voice, and other non-verbal communication. This is especially important in open relationships, where one partner may feel pressured to go along with something their partner requests, such as wanting to spend the weekend with another partner or wanting to have unprotected sex with another partner. In these situations, a partner may say yes but all their non-verbal signals are saying no, and it is imperative to "hear" that non-verbal communication and address your partner's misgivings directly. Usually, this involves either suggesting a compromise, or agreeing to postpone this request until your partner can verbalize their feelings and problem-solve to make your partner feel safer. Many couples have created major drama and pain by ignoring all the nonverbal signs that something was not really okay, even though the partner ostensibly agreed to it. Remember that people often "vote with their feet," regardless of what they say with their mouths.

In addition to your partner's words and body language, pay close attention to what they actually do after they agree to something. Their behavior often will reveal their true feelings, especially if they went along with something under duress but are not comfortable with it.

A few examples:

Your partner says yes to your request to start an outside relationship, but then vetoes the new partner for some rather dubious reason, makes rules that are so unreasonable that the potential lover loses interest, or manipulates scheduling to keep their partner from successfully making dates with anyone.

Your partner agrees that you can spend more time with an outside partner, but then sulks when you returns home from dates, or sabotages the time you spend with another partner by phoning frequently during the date or by picking a fight just before you leave for a date.

You can save everyone a lot of anguish by paying close attention to, and immediately addressing, your partner's words, nonverbal communication, and behaviors.

Step Three: Know what you want and need, and communicate it directly to your partner

Assessing your needs can be challenging. Ascertaining what we need in an open relationship is an ongoing process. Often, trial and error is the only path to discovering what boundaries and rules we may need.

You may think it is fine to consent to your partner's request to pursue sex and romance with a new lover. However, when they actually go out on that first date, you may experience panic, despair, or rage. It may take a while to pinpoint what is distressing about this situation and what will help you feel safe and loved. It may be that this particular person triggers jealousy for some reason, or you may be having difficulties because of other stresses in life, or you may be going through a lot of conflict in the relationship already and don't want the additional stress of this new partner right now.

Take responsibility for your needs. Once you are able to discern what you want, directly but gently express these needs to your partner, acknowledging that you did consent but have found that you need a change in the agreement, since this is creating more pain than you can tolerate right now.

Have some compassion for yourself and your partner. As you go through this stressful and unpredictable process, each change will create some inconvenience and distress for everyone – so cut yourselves some slack! In my experience, this is one of the most difficult parts of negotiation an open relationship, as it is very challenging for each person to develop their own guidelines that allow them to navigate these uncharted waters, and still more difficult for each partner to adjust to and accommodate those boundaries.

Relationship agreements are sometimes a "moving goalpost." Many people want an agreement that is set in stone, and will not change. For most open relationships, that is not realistic: our needs and tolerance may change, and we may need to modify the guidelines over time. This can cause resentments and disappointment for everyone along the way, especially if a partner agrees to something and cannot actually handle it. To the partner with an outside relationship, this may feel like "going backwards," because you're asking for more time and greater freedom to pursue the outside relationship, while your primary partner may be asking you to give up some of the things that you've agreed on, as they can't tolerate as much as they originally thought.

A few examples:

Jose agreed to allow his primary partner, Peter, to have sex with a previous boyfriend, Gregg,who was going to be in town for a week on business. They agreed that Peter and Gregg could spend three nights together, since Gregg would only be in town for a short time. After the first night, Jose was distraught and asked Peter to come home. Peter was angry because Jose had "broken his agreement," but they were able to make a new agreement that Peter could have two nights with Gregg instead of three.

Joan consented to Bill having sex with and spending the night with Robin. Bill had two dates with Robin, but Joan experienced intense jealousy and couldn't sleep. She asked him to continue the relationship but not to stay overnight, until she could get her anxieties under control. Both Bill and Robin felt it was unfair to rescind the agreement – but after a few more dates, Joan felt comfortable enough for Bill to spend the night with Robin again.

Yasmin and Lenny opened up their marriage, and agreed to have only casual sex with other partners. However, Yasmin found this arrangement very unsatisfying, and wanted to develop an ongoing secondary relationship with someone else. Lenny accused her of lying and manipulating him by promising only to have casual sex.Yasmin explained that she thought that would be enough, but discovered that she needed some emotional connection to enjoy sex.

Two key steps to communicating your needs to your partner

When in doubt, make sure to cover these two components when you need to renegotiate an agreement:

- Acknowledge that you have guessed wrong about what you want or what you can handle.

- Tell the truth about your needs, even though you know your partner will not be happy with what you are asking for.

Don't be tempted to tell your partner what they want to hear! It is better to be honest about your feelings and ask as clearly as possible for what you need, and be willing to compromise, rather than going along with something that you know will not work for you. The trick is knowing what your bottom line is and sticking to that, while making your best guess about when you can stretch yourself and tolerate something that is uncomfortable but not impossible.

Exercise Twenty-six: "What will work for me?"

When faced with a difficult decision on polyamorous boundaries, ask yourself these three questions (write in your answers):

What would be absolutely ideal for me in this situation? _____

_____

_____

What would be difficult and painful, but possibly manageable with some work on my part and support from my partner and other resources?_

_____

_____

What would make me really unhappy and be really impossible to accept in this situation? _____

_____

_____

Don't hesitate to say "no" to any relationship guideline or boundary that fails the last question. You may feel a lot of pressure from your partner or your partner's other partner to make more compromises or go along with something they really want, and many people try to "be a good sport," "be more flexible," "challenge yourself for your own personal growth." However, if you accept something that makes you feel fundamentally unsafe, mistreated or unloved, it will cause more harm than good.

If you are uncertain whether a specific request is tolerable for you, negotiate a fallback, so that you have a way to re-open the discussion if it proves too difficult. For instance, you can agree to try something for a month and then re-evaluate. Or you can agree to accept a range of behaviors with the caveat that if any one of them becomes too painful, you can veto one of the practices for now. Again, clear and honest communication is imperative to express what is working and what is too difficult.

Advanced communication techniques for people in open relationships

The two basic communication techniques described earlier in this chapter can be extremely helpful in communicating with your partner about your feelings and needs in an open relationship. Be patient with yourself and your partner as you practice, practice, practice good communication: it takes time and effort. Being willing to give your partner the benefit of the doubt, and assuming a positive intention, can build trust and make you both feel supported.

Once you feel more confident in your ability to communicate about your relationship, you're ready for advanced communication techniques. While these three techniques are not complicated, they can be surprisingly difficult, because most of us are not used to thinking and talking about these issues. They require being vulnerable and taking emotional risks, but are well worth the effort. You can increase the odds of success by working on these exercises when your relationship feels more stable, and by asking your partner to commit to working on them together.

Exercise Twenty-seven: Tell the truth!

You may wonder why telling the truth is an advanced technique. The fact is that most people have no experience in telling their partner the truth about other sexual and romantic relationships. Most people find it extremely difficult to tell their partner they are attracted to someone else or are becoming sexually or romantically involved with someone else. The appropriate amount of disclosure is very crucial, so that your partner knows what is happening and how it will affect them. And each person has a different constellation of needs for privacy and for information. Creating the right balance between allowing each person and each relationship to have some privacy, while providing all partners with enough information to feel safe and informed, can be complicated.

Step One: Don't lie to your partner!

While this may seem ridiculously obvious, almost everyone in open relationships has lied to a partner in one or more situations.

Why do people lie, despite their best intentions? We have never had any training in how to talk with a partner about another concurrent relationship, and it seems so counterintuitive to do so that our default programming is to lie about it. We have no model for this behavior; the only model we see is to "cheat" and lie about it. It is almost impossible for us to imagine actually telling a partner about another sexual relationship and having them respond positively.

Step Two: Practicing will make it easier to tell the truth.

It can help to practice this skill in a non-charged situation, when there is no outside relationship going on. Some couples practice by telling each other about random people they find attractive, such as strangers on the street or movie stars, just to get in the habit of talking about this subject. Others practice by talking about the romance, attractions, and sex in past relationships, since it can be less threatening to your partner to hear about relationships that are in the past.

Step Three: Tips to avoid an "honesty malfunction" under pressure

When a partner is anxious or jealous, they may ask you a question you don't want to answer, or request information you would rather keep private. There is a very strong temptation to lie at that moment, to appease them or calm their distress. Three more honest ways to address this situation are:

1. Be clear, neutral, and direct: "I understand your desire to know more, but I don't feel comfortable disclosing that," or "I want you to have as much information as possible, but my other partner would prefer I don't share that information with you."

2. Ask your partner why they want this information. See if they can identify what they hope to achieve through finding out more, and how having this information will help them. This question usually leads to a more fruitful discussion about your partner's needs and their motivation for asking for more disclosure. Usually, you'll find that there is another way to reassure them without sharing this specific information.

3. Try to answer the underlying concern instead of the superficial questions. Usually, if someone demands a lot of detailed information, what they really want to know is this: "Is this other relationship a threat to the stability or survival of my relationship? Am I in danger of being displaced or replaced by this other person?" If you can answer that question honestly and reassure your partner that they are safe and loved, their need for constant updates is likely to subside. Often, a jealous or insecure partner will ask a lot of questions and want a lot of data on any outside relationship in order to piece together as complete a picture as possible, so they can see if the outside relationship is undermining the primary relationship. If you can respond to their very primal fears of abandonment and scarcity, all the other questions become irrelevant.

Step Four: What to do if you "goof" and tell a lie

If you are caught off-guard by questioning, and react by saying things that aren't true, don't panic! Many people have done this when they felt defensive or just didn't know how to handle a partner's demands. As soon as you realize you have told some half-truths or untruths, or as soon afterward as you can muster the courage, tell your partner that you have made a mistake and that you need to correct it. This takes a lot of integrity, but it is worth coping with your partner's hurt and anger. You will cause much more damage by letting a lie stand (and pay a much higher price for it later) than by just correcting the mistake now.

Step Five: More communication is usually better than less

It's better to err on the side of too much communication rather than too little, since open relationships are complex, there are so many issues to resolve, and there can be numerous people's needs to balance. But don't process your relationship to death. Be careful not to spend all your dates having heavy discussions about your relationship! Some poly people become "process queens" and spend so much time talking about the relationship that they don't have time to actually experience and enjoy the relationship.

Exercise Twenty-eight: Learn to metacommunicate!

Philosopher Gregory Bateson coined the term "metacommunicate" in the 1970s to describe "communicating about communication." People often have different goals when they communicate. This is an especially useful concept for open relationships. If you communicate the goal of your communication to your partner before you start talking about the subject itself, this gives your partner an idea of what you are trying to achieve with this discussion, greatly increasing the likelihood that you will communicate successfully.

In working with clients over the years, it has become clear to me that whenever someone communicates with their partner, they are trying to achieve one of these five goals:

1. talking just to connect with their partner

2. asking for support or comfort

3. telling a story or relaying information

4. making a decision together

5. solving a problem together

This exercise will give you practice in meta-communicating.

Step One: Ask yourself: what is the goal of this communication?

Think of something you want to communicate to your partner, and think about what you hope to achieve by delivering that communication. Tell your partner which of these five goals your communication is trying to achieve, and have them confirm that they understand the goal. Then start talking with your partner just as you normally would about this subject. You may be surprised at how much more your partner will "get" what you are trying to say, and they are much more likely to respond with your desired outcome.

Step Two: Be aware of the influence of your gender training on your communication style

Because of our gender training, men and women often communicate with different goals. For heterosexual couples, the woman is often communicating to connect with her partner, ask for support, or relay information, and the man responds with the goal of making a decision or solving a problem – thus, neither goal is achieved. This dynamic often still exists in same-sex couples, but is usually not as pronounced, as both partners have been socialized to communicate in similar ways.

A few examples of different goals in communication:

Cathy came home from work talking about an unpleasant interaction with her boss, wanting nurturing and support from Joseph. Joseph interpreted it as a problem to be solved, making numerous suggestions on how she could have handled the situation with her boss differently in order to create a more positive outcome. Cathy felt invalidated, criticized, and defensive, and Joseph was baffled and hurt because his sensible advice and attempts to help were being rejected.

Jesse told Keira about feeling dissatisfied with his job, hoping to get input from her about whether to quit his job. He wanted her help weighing the various factors in this decision, but instead she praised him for his hard work and skills and told him how much she appreciated him. He felt frustrated because she derailed him from his focus on decision-making, but she felt hurt because he rejected her support.

Now for a successful example:

Benjamin decided to metacommunicate with his partner Molly. He started by saying, "I'd like your help in making a decision about my partner Jim, but I also want to express my feelings and be understood. And I want to hear your feelings and address any concerns you have." Molly responded that she would try to listen and give her honest feedback. Benjamin continued, "Jim would like to stop using condoms and become fluid-bonded. It would mean a lot to him and allow him to feel more intimate with me. He feels like he is being distrusted and seen as a vector of disease. He does not have any other partners now and has recently been re-tested and is negative for all STI's. I have mixed feelings about this, but since Jim and I have been lovers for three years now, it seems like a reasonable request." Molly responded, "I can understand why you and Jim would want this, and why he feels his isn't being treated fairly. I also have some anxieties about being at risk for HIV, as I don't know Jim's history." Benjamin responded, "I don't believe it would put you or me at risk, as I trust Jim to tell me if he sleeps with any new partners, and we could reconsider this then." Molly responded, "I'm not sure I'm ready to make this decision. As a compromise, could we put this on the back burner for a month and see how we both feel after that?" Benjamin suggested, "Let's wait on making a decision, and talk about it again in a couple of weeks after we both have had time to think about it more." Because Benjamin started the conversation by stating clearly the goals of the communication, it was much easier for both him and Molly to hear each other and work towards a mutually satisfying solution.

Exercise Twenty-nine: Clarify whether your communication is a request for support or action

Inappropriate level of disclosure, either too much information or not enough, is the most common communications problem in poly relationships. The second most common is mixed messages about what someone is asking for.

Here is the usual scenario: You are experiencing distress over your partner's other relationship. You express your feelings, and your partner misconstrues the goal of that communication. Communication then completely breaks down, with neither person feeling heard or respected. The crux of the confusion is this: Do you just want to express your feelings and receive support and be acknowledged for doing something very difficult, or are you asking for a change in your partner's behavior or a change in your relationship agreement?

Step one: Avoid mixed messages through clarifying your request

Before having a discussion of your distress, think about what you are asking for. Clarify your immediate goal: are you

1. expressing feelings and wanting support and compassion, or

2. requesting a change in behavior or a change in your relationship agreements?

It may be difficult to be sure what you are feeling right now, but try your best to decide whether you have a more urgent need for affirmation, support, and appreciation, or for your partner to promise to behave differently in the future.

Step Two: Identify what you need most right now

If you realize that your primary need is for love and support, try to pinpoint what you want from your partner: affection, words of endearment, being nurtured with a backrub or being taken out for breakfast, being complimented or thanked for your efforts to handle this difficult situation?

If you become clear that your request is action-oriented, try to identify what isn't working right now in your open relationship and what change you want to see. For instance, you might start by expressing your feelings: "It's lonely here without you, and I feel so neglected and abandoned when you are at your girlfriend's house!" Then, it is crucial to add, "I think maybe we should modify our relationship agreement from you spending two nights a week with her, to one night a week," or "I need you to spend more quality time with me, too, so let's make a commitment to have special date nights every Friday night." This way your partner gets a clear message that not only do you need compassion and active support, but there is a specific request for an action step. Then they can think about your request and resolve it through discussion and negotiation.

An example:

Melissa and John are a bisexual couple in a committed relationship. John also has a relationship with Ricardo. Their agreement is that John can spend two weeknights with Ricardo each week. He negotiates with Melissa to spend the weekend with Ricardo for the first time. She agrees, trying to stretch herself because she knows how important it is to them. When John returns home Monday morning after a wonderful weekend with Ricardo, Melissa breaks down crying, saying how lonely and sad she was and how she couldn't sleep. John says, "But you agreed to it, and now you're complaining about it! Well, since you're freaking out, I won't spend a weekend with him again."

She tries to explain that she just wants support and wants some gratitude for doing something really hard for her, but John thinks she wants to change their agreement back to "No weekends with Ricardo." John finally gets it when she repeats clearly, "I want you to continue spending one weekend a month with Ricardo. I just want you to hold me and acknowledge that this is really hard for me and give me some credit for my efforts."

The Jealousy Workbook

Chapter Fifteen:

Disclosure about other relationships: How much do you really want to know about your partner's other relationships?

One of the most common problems in open relationships is giving each other either too much information or not enough information about outside relationships.

Issues about disclosure about other relationships are extremely challenging in open relationships. There are several steps to addressing disclosure, and each step in the process is fraught with peril. It is very difficult for each individual to get clarity about how much they really want to know about their partner's other partners. Even when someone knows exactly what level of disclosure is ideal, their partner may not be willing to provide it. And you may feel comfortable with a certain level of disclosure in one situation but feel a need for much more (or much less) information with another partner, because of the complex constellation of different feelings and fears about particular relationships. My best advice is to proceed slowly and with caution, and don't hesitate to modify your agreements as needed.

Exercise Thirty: Which type of poly person are you?

My experience is that there area two types of polyamorous people when it comes to how much disclosure they want: those that want as much information as possible and want to know everything about their partner's other lovers and what is going on in those relationships, and those who want very little information about outside relationships.

Step One: Do you want to know everything?

For many people in open relationships, knowledge is power and having more information makes them feel safer. A lack of information makes them feel vulnerable, helpless, and out of control. The more they know about their partner's other relationships, the more secure they feel. This reassures them that they know where they stand with their partner and how their relationship fits into the bigger picture. They feel less anxious about possible surprises or reversals of fortune if they are keeping close track of what is going on with other relationships, and how that may affect them. They are sometimes so frightened of missing important information that they are tempted to read their partner's emails, hack into their phone records to see who they are calling and how often, and read their texts. While this may temporarily relieve their anxiety, it is an unacceptable invasion of privacy and usually damages a relationship by breaching trust.

Step Two: Clarify the goal of disclosure

If this description sounds like you, you can help yourself and your partner by getting clarity on your goal. This phenomenon is discussed in Exercise Twenty-eight, "Tell the truth!" It usually makes more sense to express your underlying concern than to ask a lot of superficial questions.

Usually, a demand for detailed information really means that you want to know: "Am I in danger of being displaced or replaced by this other person?" If you want reassurance that your relationship is safe and that you are loved, ask for that directly. This may relieve your need for constant updates and information.

Step Three: What if you don't want to know anything?

Some partners, on the other hand, prefer to have very little information about their partners' other relationships. In Exercise 24, I explained that some people "compartmentalize" by consciously avoiding any exposure to their partner's other relationships, as this strategy helps them manage their jealousy. Having more information only floods their minds with painful images of their partner with another lover. Hearing more about the relationship only convinces them the it must be really serious since you are talking about it so much, and each time you bring it up they fear you are going to break up with them.

Does this sound like you? The less you think about what your partner may be doing with anyone else, the safer you feel, and life goes on more smoothly and comfortably. You work to compartmentalize their other relationships and keep your focus on your relationship and your life activities.

Step Four: Educate your partner about your coping style

You may have to explain to your partner that when it comes to disclosure, less is better for you. They may feel convinced that it is healthy to talk about their other relationships frequently, and may disclose way too much, but this will only inflame the situation. This does not mean that your partner should lie to you or omit disclosing important changes in the status of an outside relationship or the development of a new sexual relationship. But they should use discretion in how much to talk about outside partners and how much detail to provide. While transparency is a valued attribute in open relationships, your partner should respect your unique set of needs regarding levels of disclosure.

Step Five: When a double standard of disclosure is appropriate

Polyamorous people seem to fall into these two camps in their needs for disclosure, because of their opposite coping strategies for handling potentially distressing information. Many couples find that one person in the couple wants a high level of disclosure, and the other partner compartmentalizes and wants minimal information. In these cases, it is fine to have a double standard of disclosure. One partner will give the other much more information about outside relationships, because that is what makes them most comfortable, and the other will in turn give their partner a very small amount of information, because they don't want to hear very much. This is one place where the "golden rule" doesn't work. "Do unto others as you would have them do unto you" is generally a good adage, but when it comes to disclosure, a better rule would be "Do unto others what they actually want and ask for."

Exercise Thirty-one: How do you guess what you want to know?

Despite their best efforts, many people guess wrong about how much they need to know. They demand a lot of information, but what they hear causes such distress that they wish they never asked. This makes a partner very reluctant to disclose much the next time, for fear of a repeat performance.

Step One: Think carefully before asking for information

Whenever you have the urge to ask your partner questions about their other relationships, stop and think about how the answer is likely to make you feel. A good rule of thumb is to try ask for less information than you think you need. Try to remember how you have felt in the past when learning similar information.

Some examples:

Fern made the mistake of asking her wife Maddy if her new lover was good in bed. This discussion revealed that the new girlfriend had some specific sexual skills. Fern was devastated and became very insecure about her desirability.

Colin asked his wife what she liked most about her new boyfriend. Alice replied that he was very intellectual and they had interesting talks about politics. Colin became convinced that Alice thought he was stupid and boring.

It is often difficult to know which pieces of information will be helpful and which will exacerbate jealousy. As one woman said to her husband, "If your new girlfriend gives better blowjobs than I do, I'm happy for you, but please don't tell me about it, because it will only make me feel insecure. And if she's rich or famous, please keep that to yourself, because it will only make me feel inadequate."

For some people, any details amount to Too Much Information and will only conjure disturbing images of their partner with someone else, convincing them that they don't measure up when compared to this new person. For others, having their partner share this feels intimate and is a bonding experience. It can even create the "sexual spillover effect," because talking about their other relationships can be sexually arousing.

Step Two: What is your bottom line of disclosure?

Because the issue of disclosure is so complex and has such potential to create crises and drama, I encourage you to come up with your own individual list of what information you need, and when you need to know it, so you can communicate this clearly to your partners and negotiate a mutually satisfactory agreement.

For most people, these are the four broad categories of what they need to know.

1. **Have you been involved in a sexual situation with this person, or do you intend to become sexual with them?** The term "sexual situation" can be more clear than "Did you have sex with them?" There are many definitions of "sex" and many misunderstandings occur over whether someone actually had sex with an outside partner. Former President Bill Clinton said, "I did not have sex with that woman," because he had received fellatio to orgasm but did not have vaginal intercourse. I have heard similar statements that "we just fooled around," or "it was only oral," or "we were making out," or "she just gave me a hand job." The partner feels deceived and betrayed. As a result, I suggest the term "sexual situation," as it includes anything that could be defined as sexual activity. Asking your partner this question means, "Did you do anything physical with this person that you would not do with a platonic friend?" This includes kissing, touching of any part of the body that could be construed as sexual (breasts, buttocks, clitoris, vagina, penis, anus), making out, getting naked together, using sex toys, having oral sex, manual sex, mutual masturbation, and vaginal or anal intercourse.

2. **Is this an ongoing romantic or sexual relationship or is it over?** Most people want to know even if it is a casual, one-time sexual experience with someone they will never see again, others only want to know if it may become an ongoing relationship. Clearly, if it's over, it may be much easier to accept it and move on. Think carefully about how you will feel if your partner does not tell you about a one-night stand or brief fling while on a trip, or whether hearing about it will create unnecessary pain for you.

3. **If it is ongoing, what is the status of this new relationship?** This is one of the most important things that most people need to know: what is the nature of this new relationship, and and what role will this new person play in their partner's life? Is this a casual sex partner or play partner? Is this a "fuck buddy" or "friend with benefits?" Is this an ongoing secondary relationship? Is this becoming serious, or even potentially a primary relationship?

4. **How will this affect me?** Naturally, most people want to know whether this new relationship, whether casual or serious, may impact their lives. Will it mean that your partner will have less time for you, whether you will be getting less attention or less sex, or whether it will just make it more complicated scheduling dates because there is another person's schedule to take into consideration? Does this new person have an STI that may behoove you to change your sexual practices with your partner? Has this new relationship changed how your partner feels about you, or altered your role in their life? Often in the beginning it is difficult to answer these questions accurately, because it is too soon to tell. It's reasonable to expect your partner to keep you informed of new developments, as they are likely to affect you.

Sex, or the intention of having sex, is the dividing line where most people really need some disclosure. Some people have asked, "Why does my partner need to know if I have had sex with someone else?" The reason is that this is a significant piece of news: something new and different is going on in their partner's life that may affect them. Most people want to know even if it is a casual, one-time sexual experience.

Step Three: When do you want to know?

Another area of conflict is not just how much you want to know but when you want to know it. Take this brief quiz about the timing of disclosure. When do you want your partner to tell you about a new person in their lives?

a) before they have sex with another person?

b) when they first begin to "court" a potential new partner, when they first flirt or exchange phone numbers or send each other emails?

c) when they first develop an attraction towards someone but before you ask them for a date or reveal your interest to them?

d) just before the first date?

e) after the first date?

f) after they first have sex with the new person?

g) when they decide to have an ongoing relationship?

There is no right or wrong answer to this quiz, as each person will feel comfortable with a different set of parameters. And within a couple, each partner may have different needs, so having a double standard of disclosure may be necessary. The goal is to balance each partner and each relationship's optimal level of disclosure with each partner's need for privacy and agency.

Politically incorrect note about the timing of disclosure

While generalizations based on gender are always dangerous, there is enough of a trend to warrant a mention. Women are more likely to want to be told as soon as their partner becomes romantically interested in someone else, and often feel deceived if their partner doesn't mention anything until there is a courtship underway and a date planned. I have heard many women say, "Why didn't you tell me you were emailing her and calling her?" Often the exasperated man will say things like, "We haven't even met!" or "We've just been emailing, there's nothing going on!" However, because many women are much more concerned about their partner's level of emotional intimacy with another woman than about whether they have actually had a date or had sex, the fact that some courtship has occurred without their knowledge makes them feel betrayed.

Other women just want to know about an outside partner before any sexual activity is initiated. This confuses men, because they have no idea when or if sex will occur.

Some examples:

One man explained, "I met a woman at a poly event, and we went on four dates, but I couldn't tell if she just wanted to be friends. I told my wife that it was platonic. Then she invited me over to her house for lunch, and she initiated sex. I told my wife as soon as I got home, and she said I lied about it being platonic. But we were just friends until she asked me to go to bed with her."

Some couples make an agreement that they will tell each other if they are attracted to someone or have "sexual intentions" towards someone new. However, some men find this requirement untenable. Josh explained, "I meet women every day who I would sleep with, given the opportunity, but most of the time nothing is going to happen! I am not going to tell my partner every time I meet a sexually attractive woman. Why put my partner through some anxiety and asking me a million questions, when nothing is likely to come of it?"

Bob said, "What if it doesn't work out? It's bad enough to be sexually rejected. I don't want to have to go back to my partner after a date and tell them they got all jealous for no reason because this woman doesn't want to sleep with me!"

Linda said, "I need to know as soon as possible after Karen has sex with a new person. She has some 'wiggle room' in the interests of picking an ideal time to tell me."

Ingrid said, "Once he informs me that he is having sex with someone new, he doesn't need to tell me again about the fact that they are having a sexual relationship. I will assume that the sex will continue to be a part of that relationship, until he tells me it's no longer sexual."

And most men want to know immediately if their partner has had sex with someone else, but until and unless sex takes place, they don't want to hear about the courtship. Ben said that his partner Jennifer frequently corresponded with both women and men by email on dating websites. Ben told her to stop telling him every time she was interested in someone, since it made him anxious and jealous, and then usually nothing happened. "Just let me know if you actually have sex!"

For some men, there is no need to know anything until it is clear that the outside relationship will affect them. One man explained, "My wife travels on business and goes to conferences, and often has fun adventures when she is out of town. It's a one-time fling and she will never see the person again, so why should I grill her about it and get jealous? However, if she really connects with someone and is going to stay in touch with them, then I want to know what's going on."

Step Four: What if the relationship is ongoing?

If the relationship goes on for a significant period of time, most people are likely to want further disclosure, about these four issues:

1. What does this other person mean to my partner?

2. What does my partner receive in this other relationship?

These first two questions are asked not so much for yourself. Rather, because you feel connected to your partner, you want to know about something important going on in their life, and why this is significant for them. If your partner got very involved in an activity such as a new job, a political organization, community service, or a new hobby, you would want to understand what was compelling for them about that experience. Similarly, you want to know what an outside relationship means to your partner and how it enhances their life. You don't really need to know for your own well-being, but rather because you want to understand your partner. They have the right to tell you if they want more privacy around this issue, and they may limit what you hear.

These next two questions are crucial for your understanding of the potential impact of this relationship on you. Unlike the first two questions, it is imperative that your partner be transparent in disclosing what is happening in their other relationship that will affect the health and stability of your relationship. This is particularly true if the other relationship is beginning to absorb more of your partner's time and attention, and you have any evidence that your own relationship is suffering.

3. How is this relationship affecting your feelings for me?

4. What future do you see for this relationship and how will that affect our relationship?

Penny described the first two questions as "want to know" and the last two questions as "need to know." As she said, "I am curious and would love to know the answers to all four questions, as this would help me know my partner better and feel closer to her. But I respect her need for privacy and I only insist on the answers to the last two questions, because they could have a major impact on my life."

The Jealousy Workbook

Chapter Sixteen:

What's compersion got to do with it?

What is compersion? You may have heard the term "compersion" bandied about by people in open relationships, and you may not be quite sure what it means or how it happens. The basic definition of compersion is that it is a combination of pleasant thoughts and feelings you experience towards your partner when they are in a positive romantic or sexual relationship with someone else. Because you love your partner and want them to be happy, it is at least theoretically possible that you can experience joy in knowing they are enjoying another relationship in addition to their relationship with you.

"Good luck with that!" Most people laugh out loud when they first hear the concept of compersion, as it seems so completely absurd and counter-intuitive that we could ever feel anything good about our partner sleeping with someone else. When one woman first heard someone waxing rhapsodic about how she "should" feel all warm and fuzzy when her partner loves someone new, her response was, "Good luck with that! I'm too busy suppressing my revenge fantasies and restraining myself from going nuclear on their ass to have any feelings of compersion!"

Most people share similar reactions to the idea of compersion: the anxiety and pain of jealousy is so strong that it is crowding out any possible positive feelings. When someone feels threatened, as we usually do when a partner sleeps with someone else, we are so consumed with protecting our precious relationship that there is no energy available for compersion to emerge. And for those who tend to be extremely jealous, it seems impossible to imagine that we would be jumping for joy over our partner's hot love affair with someone else. If you feeling frightened, angry, and/or sad over your partner's romantic interest in someone else, how could you possibly be happy for them?

What prevents compersion? While there is no guarantee that anything we do will magically create compersion, we can remove the obvious obstacles that prevent it from happening. Because our immediate experience in this situation is usually one of intense loss and grief, our reaction is feeling deprivation and scarcity rather than generosity and enthusiasm for our partner's new love affair. As one woman put it, "When my girlfriend told me she was falling in love with a new woman, I felt like I was starving to death: she was taking some of her love and giving it to someone else. How could she expect me to feel happy for her that this other woman was eating a delicious meal right in front of me while I was going hungry? I literally felt like she was taking food off my plate and giving it to someone else."

A man whose wife began a long-distance relationship with another man described it in similar terms of scarce resources: "I realized that I saw our love in some weird way as a cosmic bank account with a certain amount of money in it, and that love was a finite resource. I felt like I had earned that love over the years of our relationship, like earning money and putting it in the bank. When she started a relationship with this other man, it was like she took the money I had worked so hard to earn, withdrew it from our joint bank account, and then gave it away to this other guy."

Scarcity will always trump compersion. As a result, we need to feel we are getting "enough" love and attention before we can hope to feel good about our partner having other lovers.

Exercise Thirty-two: Moving from constriction to expansion

One way to work towards feeling compersion is to see jealousy as a "constricted" state, and trying to move towards a more "expansive" state. Dr. Dave Doleshal, a psychologist working with people in open relationships, has conceptualized jealousy as a state which compels us to "constrict," to shut down, protect, set boundaries, and hold to a rigid view of the current situation. Because we experience jealousy as a threat to our relationship, we go into a "siege mentality" which tells us to bar the doors, get out our weapons, and hunker down for a battle. This puts us in such a hypervigilant posture that we are primed to fight rather than to problem-solve.

Dr. Doleshal encourages clients in a jealousy state to deliberately try to override some of that constriction to move towards an expansive state, one that is more open, curious, trusting, and flexible, to find solutions. This is easier said than done! Here are some tips to make it a little more possible to experience more expansion and compersion and less constriction and jealousy.

Step One: Notice the physical symptoms of constriction

In a constricted state, the ancient reptilian part of our brain erroneously believes that our life is literally at stake, so all options narrow to focus on survival. Being in this state of vigilance is so painful and frightening that it's hard to imagine any way out. If, however, you train yourself to notice the signs of constriction in your body, your mind, and your emotions, you may be able to learn to modify that state and create additional options. When you first notice that you are feeling jealous, check in with yourself right away to notice your physical body – asking yourself these questions to help you identify when you are experiencing a constricted state:

- Are your jaws clenched? Is your tongue pressed against the roof of your mouth? If so, deliberately part your top teeth from your bottom teeth slightly and allow your tongue to fall forward slightly away from the back of your throat and away from the roof of your mouth. Let your jaws drop down as loosely as possible. Repeat whenever you feel that tightness in back of your jaws.

- Look in the mirror to see if you are frowning and if the muscles around your eyes are tight and making creases in your forehead. To release that tension, close your eyes for a moment and gently raise your eyebrows as far as they will go and then let them fall back down naturally.

- How does your neck feel right now? Gently and slowly turn your head as far as you can to the left side, then back to center, and then as far to the right as you can. If your neck feels sore and stiff, turn your head a few more times very gently from side to side to release the tension. Lean your head to the left as if you are trying to touch your left ear to your shoulder. Then lean to the right as if you are trying to touch your right ear to your right shoulder. Feel the muscles loosening along the sides of your neck.

- Are you aware of any tightness or pain in the muscles connecting your neck and your shoulders? Deliberately shrug your shoulders, trying to raise them as high as possible toward your ears, then let them drop back down. We tend to tense up our shoulders and carry them too close to our ears, rather than letting them hang down in a relaxed comfortable way. Repeat "the shrug" throughout the day whenever you feel your neck and shoulders tensing up.

- Notice your breathing, and see if you can tell if you are breathing from your chest or from your abdomen. Chest breathing tends to be more rapid and shallow, creating a more constricted state by keeping the breath too tight. Trying to consciously take some deep breaths, pushing the breath down into the abdomen, can have a very relaxing effect, and is the basis of most forms of meditation.

- How do the muscles in your stomach and abdomen feel right now? Do you notice any soreness in the upper abdomen, just below the ribcage? This soreness can be caused by inadvertently tightening the muscles in your stomach and abdomen, or by shallow breathing. You may be able to relieve that discomfort through better posture, sitting or standing up straighter, and by slowly breathing into the sore spots to relax the muscles.

- Notice the muscles in your hips and buttocks, and become aware of any tightness or pain in those areas. Many people hold a lot of tension in those muscles, often created by sitting too much, due to working at a computer or a sedentary lifestyle. Massage, yoga or other stretches, and getting some vigorous exercise can help reverse the pattern of pelvic tightness.

- Are you clenching your fists or noticing tightness in your fingers or hands? You may find it helpful to deliberately clench your fists, then open your hands outward and allow your arms and hands to hang down by your sides, to relax all the muscles in your hands and arms.

The importance of relaxation

Any activity that encourages relaxation can help alleviate the physical state of tension that is present during a constricted state. Meditation, guided imagery, self-hypnosis, relaxation CDs and downloads, yoga, walking, swimming, gardening, knitting or crafting, being in nature, massage, listening to music, a hot cup of tea, or a soothing conversation with a friend can all "retrain" your body to stay more relaxed and avoid tightening up so much. If you have a medical condition that causes physical pain and contracted muscles, your health care practitioner may suggest medication or other treatment to relieve this tightness.

Step Two: Recognize and counteract a constricted mental and emotional state

A jealousy experience can create a constricted mental and emotional state, as well as physical pain and tightness. This state typically involves rigid "black and white thinking" with no room for nuance, obsessive thoughts that seem impossible to push out of your head, exaggerated fears, and a pessimistic view of the future. When any of these happen, a strong effort may be required to counteract these thoughts and feelings. This usually requires a two-step process: first, confronting the obsessive and thoughts and self-critical feelings to see if they contain any kernel of truth, and second, taking steps to take care of yourself, in order to ease out of a constricted state into a more expansive state.

Start by noticing what thoughts are rushing around in your head when you feel jealous, and especially the repetitive thoughts that keep recurring. Write these thoughts down, and circle the appropriate answer as to whether these statements are likely to be true, false, or have some kernel of truth but not be completely true. Here are a few common examples:

"He doesn't love me anymore, that's why he is dating someone else."

>   True   Contains some small kernel of truth   False

"He must think I'm pathetic and needy."

>   True   Contains some small kernel of truth   False

"I'll never be good enough for her, and I could never compete with her beautiful new lover."

>   True   Contains some small kernel of truth   False

"He's probably at her house right now seducing her."

>   True   Contains some small kernel of truth   False

"She's lying to me about her feelings for her new girlfriend."

>   True   Contains some small kernel of truth   False

"They are having unsafe sex."

>   True   Contains some small kernel of truth   False

If you are able to see that some of your thoughts do not reflect reality, tell yourself: "These are fears, not facts." Repeat that mantra whenever these specific thoughts recur, since you have ascertained that there is no kernel of truth there.

If you can see that some thoughts have a small kernel of truth but are not entirely true, see if you can separate fact from fiction, and write down a more accurate description without exaggeration or embellishment. The part that is actually true is usually much easier to handle than the dramatized version.

If you strongly believe that some of these thoughts are 100% true, call at least two friends and ask them if they agree with your assessment. If there is consensus that these thoughts and feelings are accurate, then it is probably time to sit down with your partner and share these thoughts to try to resolve them.

An example:

Bill and his partner Diego were in a long-term open relationship, living in New York. Diego developed a relationship with Jonas, who lived in Boston, where Diego routinely traveled due to his job. Whenever Diego went to Boston on business, Bill's mind was flooded with images of Diego having sex with his other partner. He couldn't sleep and didn't feel like eating. He felt desperate and alone, and the constant repetition of negative beliefs only made him feel more helpless and hopeless. He utilized this exercise by writing down his obsessive thoughts.

Constricting thought:

"I bet they're having sex day and night, and he's probably better in bed than I am!"

> True   Contains some small kernel of truth   False

He realized that the first half of this thought was probably true, because the relationship was new and they only saw each other once a month for about twenty-four hours, so it made sense that they would be having sex frequently during their short visits. As for the second part of the thought, he realized that he had no way of knowing whether Jonas was a better lover, that this was completely subjective, and that he could not control the quality of Diego and Jonas's sex life together. He reminded himself that he and Diego had a very satisfying sexual relationship, and that would not be affected by Diego's sexual relationship with Jonas.

Constricting thought: "Diego would rather be with Jonas than with me."

> True   Contains some small kernel of truth   False

He decided that there was a small kernel of truth in that thought, because Diego saw Jonas so infrequently that he was probably quite eager to see him by the time he actually got to Boston. He only spent one day with him, and spent the other twenty-nine days of the month with Bill. Looking at it from that angle took a lot of the sting out of it, reminding him that he had Diego to himself all month long, so he felt a little more generous about lending him to Jonas one day out of the month.

Constricting thought: "I'm home all alone feeling like crap, while my partner's up in Boston having this great love affair."

> True   Contains some small kernel of truth   False

In thinking about this, he realized that this was quite true, but that he had a choice about whether to stay home alone wallowing in despair. So he got on the subway and went to a gay men's support group at the LGBT Community Center, where he was able to talk about his feelings. He received a lot of feedback from the men in the group that he was attractive and lovable; they reminded him that his partner had stayed with him for twenty-five years and was very committed to him. One of them told Bill about a website about improving your self-esteem, and he tried some of the self-care and esteem-building exercises, which he found helpful.

After Diego came back from Boston the next day, Bill shared his fears of being abandoned, and Diego was able to reassure him of his love. He even joked, "Jonas is such a drama queen, last night he kept me up half the night processing about the relationship! Seeing him once a month is plenty for me!" Bill began to feel less constricted and more confident about being able to cope. The next time Diego went to Boston, Bill deliberately thought of his partner having long "processing" discussions with Jonas and focused on that image to replace the images of them having sex, and that felt much more tolerable.

Step Three: Move from exclusion, abandonment, and deprivation towards belonging, autonomy, and responsibility.

Dr. Doleshal says that when people feel in a constricted state, they usually fear one or more of these three experiences: exclusion, abandonment, or deprivation. All three are experiences that make us feel powerless and victimized. We mistakenly become convinced that our partner is responsible for our pain, and for relieving that pain.

In reality, of course, it is not nearly that simple. Our partner's actions and behaviors certainly have a huge influence on us, and can create distress for us, but we are giving away all our power if we believe they are the cause our problems and their actions can alleviate those problems. It is perfectly reasonable to ask our partner to stick to agreements, give us love and support, and listen to our feelings and needs. However, we can empower ourselves by looking at each of these three experiences and implementing self-care to meet more of our own needs.

Dr. Doleshal's advice is: "If you are feeling excluded, move towards belonging. If you are feeling abandonment, mover towards autonomy. If you are feeling deprivation, move towards responsibility." Let's look at these concepts in more detail.

Exclusion

Anyone in an open relationship can feel very left out when their partner has another partner. Being left home alone while your partner is out having fun can create resentment and envy, and may be too reminiscent of feeling slighted by parents who gave more attention to a sibling, being excluded from "the cool clique" as a teenager, or being dumped by a previous lover. This feeling can be exacerbated by your partner doing all sorts of romantic things with the new lover that they may no longer do with you: sending flowers, sending sexy or loving texts, planning elaborate dates, going for long walks.

Move toward belonging

You can move from feeling excluded to a feeling of belonging by proactively taking steps that make you feel more connected – to your partner, to your community, to your own goals and projects, and to your own strength. One woman said, "Exclusion feels to me like everybody else is inside together all warm and happy, gathered around the Christmas tree opening their presents, and I'm outside in the snow looking in the window." She felt excluded by her lover dating someone else, but realized that she had many avenues for "belonging." She had a close relationship with her mother and sister, as well as her extended family. She was well-respected at her job, and felt a sense of belonging and importance through her work. And she coached a girl's basketball team, so this too was a source of belonging to a community where she felt very needed. Whenever she felt left out by her partner being out on a date, she reminded herself that she had other options for connecting, and feeling loved and appreciated. When her partner planned dates with other lovers, he planned social events, getting together with family members or friends, or work-related activities when her partner planned dates with other lovers, tapping into her larger community.

An example:

Jorge, a bisexual man in a committed poly marriage with a woman, was completely confused when his wife got involved with Paolo, a younger, charismatic artist who was also bisexual. Jorge became intensely jealous when he saw some of her sexy and romantic text messages to Paolo, because he feared she was falling in love with him and would leave the marriage. At the same time he found the whole situation extremely exciting and sexually arousing – because he was also very attracted to Paolo, he envied his wife, and felt left out! He felt what he identified as compersion because he was happy for her having this wonderful love affair with Paolo; he just wished he could be a part of it, and feared that she would prefer Paolo over him.

What can anthropologists teach us about compersion?

Some researchers have suggested that in modern Western societies, we place way too much importance on our romantic relationships, and that we are too dependent on those relationships to provide meaning and a sense of connection. In some other cultures, a spouse or romantic relationship is only one part of the web of community that give individuals a sense of belonging and inclusion.

For instance, Dr. Leanna Wolfe is an anthropologist who has studied several rural

African cultures where polygamy is practiced – that is, it is acceptable for men to marry several wives. Dr. Wolfe describes them as "co-wives," living together in a compound where each wife has her own small house or living unit with her children. The women work together doing farming, cooking, and raising children. The husband divides his time between his wives, and is much less central to their daily routine, as their lives revolve around work, children, extended family, and community. As a result, Dr. Wolfe's research shows that they do not report feelings of exclusion when the husband is with one of the other wives, as they experience belonging and connection through their extended families and other activities.

Dr. Ralph Hupka is another anthropologist who has spent decades studying jealousy in various cultures around the world. One of his most interesting findings is that in some indigenous cultures where polygamy is practiced, "co-wives," married to the same husband, often experience a more practical form of what we would call "compersion." For instance, many wives report being happy when the husband marries an additional wife because the new wife will share the heavy workload of farming and caring for children, and will provide companionship. And one wife who was infertile was grateful to the other wives who had children, because the children would take care of her in her old age. Dr. Hupka's research also confirms that scarcity prevents compersion. He reports that co-wives report very little jealousy, but that they do become extremely jealous if the husband gives too much time, attention, or more resources to another wife and her children. For instance, jealousy occurs if the husband provides more livestock, tools, or gifts to one wife or her children than to the other wives and children. Scarcity of resources, including time

and attention as well as money and practical resources, undermines compersion.

This research indicates that being less dependent on our primary relationship can help create some form of compersion. If our love relationship is our only source of love, identity, and belonging, we are likely to feel fiercely possessive of our partner's time, romantic attention, and loyalty. Conversely, if we have more available avenues for companionship and a sense of being an integral part of a cohesive community, we are more likely to feel satisfied and secure. This allows us to experience an "expansive state," potentially including feeling more supportive of our partner's romantic relationship with someone else.

Abandonment: Most people have some feelings of abandonment when their partner starts a new relationship with someone else, feelings which often persist long after the new relationship becomes established. Feeling abandoned may seem like the same thing as feeling excluded, but there is an important difference. Exclusion is about being prevented from participating in something, feeling that someone else is being chosen to participate while you are being rejected. Abandonment involves being left alone by someone you expected to be available and attentive to your needs. Exclusion requires that your partner is connecting with someone else and choosing not to include you, whereas abandonment can simply mean your partner is withdrawing from you: you could feel abandoned if you partner just stopped interacting with you to read a book for a few hours. Carried to its most extreme, people often feel abandoned when a loved one dies, as if that person had deliberately chosen to leave them behind. So abandonment is more about feeling alone, lonely, and wanting companionship and attention.

Dr. Doleshal reminds us that abandonment is a term that more appropriately describes something an adult can do to a child, such as a father abandoning his children after a divorce, as the term implies that one person is responsible for the well-being of the other. In fact it is not really possible for an adult to be abandoned, because, unlike children, adults are fully capable of taking care of themselves. We do not actually "need" a partner to take care of us, and when we feel abandoned, we are subscribing to the myth that we are powerless and cannot survive without our partner's attention.

Dr. Doleshal advises people to "move from abandonment to autonomy." How? By becoming more independent and taking care of yourself. This requires sufficient differentiation from your partner – remembering that even though you are deeply in love, your connection to your partner continues even while they are involved in an outside relationship. Try to trust in the bond you have with your partner, knowing that your relationship is strong enough to survive these brief separations, and that you can enjoy your own independent life.

In choosing to be in an open relationship, you are giving each other the gift of freedom. You are trusting your partner to connect with others and continue to return to you, keeping your relationship intact.

"Moving towards autonomy" will look different for each person. It could mean choosing to pursue an interest: a sport, learning Spanish, political activism, doing gardening, developing a spiritual path, or going back to school. It could mean spending more time with friends, or more time at work on a special project. Or you may want to start dating someone new or developing a deeper relationship with someone you are already involved with.

If you continue to feel abandoned, you may be experiencing triggers from your past. You may have experienced true abandonment in your childhood, such as the death of a parent or a separation from a parent or important adult in your life. This situation may be too reminiscent of that very painful experience. You may benefit from counseling to separate your past experience of loss from your current relationship.

Seeing your partner as the source of your happiness puts too much pressure on the relationship. Being more independent can be empowering, making you more proactive in creating your own fulfillment.

Deprivation: Many people find the feelings of exclusion, abandonment, and deprivation to be so connected that it can be difficult to disentangle them. Understanding the distinctions between them, though, can be very helpful in reducing your jealousy and moving towards compersion.

Deprivation is a feeling of never having enough, and it is nearly impossible to feel good about a partner's other relationships if you are feeling a sense of scarcity. Dr. Doleshal suggests "moving from deprivation to responsibility," which means taking more responsibility for your own needs.

While exclusion, abandonment, and deprivation are different experiences, the solutions are similar: pursuing activities, experiences, and relationships that provide more meaning and satisfaction in your life, creating a feeling of abundance. However, Alexis misinterpreted this advice. She said with exasperation, "You're telling me to cram more into my life, when I'm already exhausted and overworked with a very demanding schedule. That's just going to make me feel more depleted." I clarified that the goal is not to add more commitments but rather to look at ways to reorganize your priorities and activities to better satisfy your needs. This will usually require dropping some activities, delegating some tasks, and possibly adding more fulfilling experiences. The idea is to decrease things that drain you, and allow time and space for rest and for "recharging your battery."

For instance, Alexis felt frustrated because her lover had a primary partner, and as a result, he could only spend one night a week with her. She worked as an emergency room nurse, and commuted in bad traffic every day. She arrived home each night feeling anxious and depressed, desperately wanting companionship. She felt overwhelmed with the responsibilities of taking care of her house and yard, and couldn't keep up with bills, shopping, and other household tasks. Spending most nights alone was very painful for her and she felt very angry at her lover's partner for not allowing them to spend more time together.

She realized that she was looking to her love relationship to somehow compensate for being depleted by her job and the tasks of everyday life. She came up with a plan. First, she rented out her spare bedroom to a friend who had just gotten divorced and lost her home due to foreclosure. Her friend paid part of the mortgage and shared in housework, cooking, and yardwork – allowing Alexis to change jobs to an emergency room at a smaller hospital much closer to home. The new job required a small cut in pay, but but she could sleep an hour later and it saved her two hours of commuting. Her new roommate loved to cook, and frequently had dinner on the table when Alexis came home from work; the hot meals and companionship filled many of the needs that she had been seeking in her love relationship. On weekends when her lover was with his primary partner, she and her roommate planted a vegetable garden in the yard, painted the house together, and enjoyed bike rides.

The solution was a two-step process: first she reduced the desperate feeling of scarcity by eliminating some of the stresses that were draining her, and secondly she created a situation that more fully met her needs for comfort, attention, and companionship.

You may discover that you are expecting a partner to meet many needs that are created outside of the relationship, and this expectation is usually not realistic. While this tendency is common in monogamous relationships, it is often magnified in open relationships – perhaps because it is tempting to believe that your dissatisfaction is caused entirely by your partner's time and energy being diverted to other partners.

Erik complained that "If only Sophia left Ben, she could spend all her time with me, and I would be so much happier." However, his past relationships had all been monogamous, and he was dissatisfied in those relationships as well. Further discussion revealed that he suffered from chronic depression, and expected a lover to take care of him. No partner had ever been able to provide the level of support, comfort, and attention that he needed, as he was far too high-maintenance. He joined a weekly support group for managing depression, and also began counseling to learn behavioral techniques for his depression. This significantly reduced his intense feelings of scarcity and need, and improved his self-esteem because he was proud of being less dependent on Sophia and more accepting of her relationship with Ben.

Another way of addressing deprivation is to systematically identify your needs, and how your relationship addresses those needs. Because deprivation can be such a painful and debilitating experience, I have developed this exercise to help you assess your relationship resources and address any areas of scarcity.

Exercise Thirty-three: Identify your relationship's scarcity and abundance quotients

Step One: Take stock of your relationship resources

Think of your relationship as a bundle of valuable resources, and identify what you receive in your relationship. For each resource on the list below, how important is it to you to receive this in your relationship? Then, on a scale of one to ten, rate how well this need is met in your relationship.

Companionship

How important is this resource to you?   1 2 3 4 5 6 7 8 9 10

How well is this need met in your relationship? 1 2 3 4 5 6 7 8 9 10

Affection and touch

How important is this resource to you?   1 2 3 4 5 6 7 8 9 10

How well is this need met in your relationship? 1 2 3 4 5 6 7 8 9 10

Sexual satisfaction and compatibility

How important is this resource to you?   1 2 3 4 5 6 7 8 9 10

How well is this need met in your relationship? 1 2 3 4 5 6 7 8 9 10

Emotional intimacy and closeness

How important is this resource to you?   1 2 3 4 5 6 7 8 9 10

How well is this need met in your relationship? 1 2 3 4 5 6 7 8 9 10

Romantic love and romantic attention

How important is this resource to you?   1 2 3 4 5 6 7 8 9 10

How well is this need met in your relationship? 1 2 3 4 5 6 7 8 9 10

Intellectual rapport and compatibility

How important is this resource to you?   1 2 3 4 5 6 7 8 9 10

How well is this need met in your relationship? 1 2 3 4 5 6 7 8 9 10

Adequate amount of quality time together

How important is this resource to you?   1 2 3 4 5 6 7 8 9 10

How well is this need met in your relationship? 1 2 3 4 5 6 7 8 9 10

Trust and emotional safety

How important is this resource to you?   1 2 3 4 5 6 7 8 9 10

How well is this need met in your relationship? 1 2 3 4 5 6 7 8 9 10

Long-term security and stability of the relationship

How important is this resource to you?   1 2 3 4 5 6 7 8 9 10

How well is this need met in your relationship? 1 2 3 4 5 6 7 8 9 10

Sense of family and community

How important is this resource to you?   1 2 3 4 5 6 7 8 9 10

How well is this need met in your relationship? 1 2 3 4 5 6 7 8 9 10

Domestic partnership (compatibility in living together or spending time together)

How important is this resource to you?   1 2 3 4 5 6 7 8 9 10

How well is this need met in your relationship? 1 2 3 4 5 6 7 8 9 10

Independence, personal autonomy, and privacy

How important is this resource to you?   1 2 3 4 5 6 7 8 9 10

How well is this need met in your relationship? 1 2 3 4 5 6 7 8 9 10

Shared interests and activities

How important is this resource to you?   1 2 3 4 5 6 7 8 9 10

How well is this need met in your relationship? 1 2 3 4 5 6 7 8 9 10

Similar values and world view

How important is this resource to you?   1 2 3 4 5 6 7 8 9 10

How well is this need met in your relationship? 1 2 3 4 5 6 7 8 9 10

Financial compatibility

How important is this resource to you?   1 2 3 4 5 6 7 8 9 10

How well is this need met in your relationship? 1 2 3 4 5 6 7 8 9 10

Step Two: Do the math to identify your "robust relationship resources"

For each of the relationship resources outlined above, now write down each one where the numbers you circled for the importance of the resource match or are closely aligned with the numbers you picked for how well this need is met.

These are clearly areas where you are experiencing abundance in your relationship. Write these resources down in the space below. These are the areas where your relationship comes closest to fulfilling your needs.

My most robust relationship resources are:

1._____

2._____

3._____

4._____

If you find that you have at least three or four areas where your have a "match," in that the resource is rated extremely high in importance to you and you also feel that need is being well-met in your relationship, there is some chance you may be able to feel a little compersion. Why? Because your love batteries are fully charged and you are experiencing enough relationship satisfaction that you may be able to stretch yourself to feel more like sharing your partner with someone else. It's easier to feel generous with your partner's time, energy, and sexual/romantic attention when you feel like there is enough to go around and you will not be short-changed.

An example:

Jenna wrote that Sex, Affection, Intellectual rapport, Sense of family, and Similar values were all 9 or 10 in importance to her, and they were all 8 or 9 in how well these needs were met in her relationship. These were her most robust relationship resources, so her core relationship needs were being satisfied. As a result, she was in a much better position to potentially experience some amount of compersion, because she was pretty satisfied in her relationship and getting "enough" of the most important resources she was seeking in a primary relationship. A feeling of abundance, or at least adequacy, and the satisfaction of our basic needs are a prerequisite for compersion to occur.

Step Three: Identify discrepancies between needs and resources

Now take another look at the entire list of relationship resources. Notice which ones show a significant difference in the number you circled for importance of this resource to you and the number you circled for how well this need is being met in your relationship. Write down below any of these resources where the two numbers are separated by at least 4 points, such as one being an 7 and the other a 3. These are the areas in your relationship where you are feeling unsatisfied, where your relationship resources are the weakest.

My weakest relationship resources are:

1.＿＿＿＿＿＿＿＿＿＿＿＿＿＿＿＿＿＿＿＿＿＿＿＿＿＿＿＿＿＿＿

2.＿＿＿＿＿＿＿＿＿＿＿＿＿＿＿＿＿＿＿＿＿＿＿＿＿＿＿＿＿＿＿

3.＿＿＿＿＿＿＿＿＿＿＿＿＿＿＿＿＿＿＿＿＿＿＿＿＿＿＿＿＿＿＿

4.＿＿＿＿＿＿＿＿＿＿＿＿＿＿＿＿＿＿＿＿＿＿＿＿＿＿＿＿＿＿＿

Step Four: Get help if the discrepancies are too extreme

If you do not have at least three relationship resources where your needs match your experience, where you rated the importance of the resource at an 8 or above and also rated the need being met at an 8 or above, you are living in a state of chronic scarcity. Your most core relationship needs are not being met in this relationship, and you and your partner need to discuss this and see why this is true. Have you been reluctant to ask your partner for what you need? Have you asked repeatedly but your partner is unable or unwilling to give you more in order to meet these needs? Is your partner spread too thin with work, outside relationships, hobbies, family obligations, and other commitments to be available for your relationship, or do you and your partner have incompatible needs? Are your expectations of a relationship unrealistic, are you demanding too much from your partner?

You and your partner may need couples counseling or some other assistance to understand why your most important relationship needs are consistently unsatisfied. You may find it helpful to attend a support group or discussion group for people in open relationships in order to learn how other people are handling these issues. You have already taken a big step by doing this exercise. There are many other books, websites, workshops, and other resources available to help you and your partner assess why there is such a big gap between what you feel you need and what you are receiving.

One thing is clear: you will not experience compersion if you feel you are not getting enough of the most important things you are seeking in an intimate relationship. You will constantly be wanting more, and will be likely to experience any time and attention your partner gives to someone else as taking something away from you, and will feel even more unsatisfied. As a result, being in an open relationship will feel like a starvation diet, and you and your partner will be locked in constant conflict over any outside relationships. This usually creates a power struggle that is draining and counterproductive, damaging your relationship and undermining trust and intimacy.

An example:

Jay and Lemont are a gay married couple. Jay complained that Lemont, a doctor with a busy private practice, was "married to his job," creating a scarcity of time and energy for their relationship. Interestingly, Jay rated many of the relationship resources very high on both counts. For instance, he rated Sexual compatibility, Affection, Independence, Domestic partnership, Financial compatibility, and Intellectual rapport as 9 or 10 in importance, as well as in those needs being well met in the relationship. However, he rated Adequate amount of quality time as a 10 in importance and a 2 in terms of how well that need was being met. As a result, he was distraught when his partner developed an ongoing fuck-buddy relationship with an attractive younger man named Nathan. Lemont felt that it added spark and intimacy to share his sexual exploits when he came home, saying, "Aren't you proud of having a husband who can still attract a hot young hunk? That's a compliment to you and your good taste!" However, because he was experiencing chronic deprivation, Jay felt only fear that the new "boy toy" would take more of his partner's time and attention away from him.

Lemont decided to hire another doctor to share his practice so he could be home in the evenings rather than at the office until 8:00 PM. This allowed them to spend a lot more time together, and Jay realized that he was no longer feeling jealous about the time Lemont spent with his other boyfriend. In fact, he began to ask Lemont more about the relationship. Jay began inviting Nathan over to their home for parties and barbecues with their friends, and to share Thanksgiving and Christmas celebrations, since Nathan was estranged from his own family. It turned out that Jay was jealous primarily of the time Nathan was receiving rather than the relationship itself. When Lemont started giving Jay more time and attention, Jay developed more compersion towards his partner's other relationship.

The Jealousy Workbook

Exercise Thirty-Four: Imagine "looking through their eyes, and being in their shoes"

One additional technique which can lead to some feelings of compersion is adapted from a Neuro-linguistic Programming™ technique designed to increase empathy and resolve conflict between individuals. This four-step process invites you to develop a broader perspective on your situation by trying to imagine what each person is experiencing.

1. Try to relax by taking three deep breaths and settling into a comfortable posture. Now, bring to mind the most recent situation which triggered your jealousy. Visualize that situation and remember all the many thoughts, feelings, and physical sensations you experienced.

2. Then try to imagine being inside your partner's body, as if you were inside their head looking out at you. Try to imagine what your partner is feeling, all the many feelings, thoughts, and sensations going on inside them about this situation, how they are feeling towards you, and how they are feeling towards their other partner. Try to empathize with any distress they may be feeling, as well as with the love and good feelings they are feeling towards you, and all the feelings, both negative and positive, they may be feeling towards their other partner. Try to imagine that you could feel their feelings, as if you could "walk a mile in their shoes."

3. Then try to stretch yourself to imagine being inside the head and heart of your parnter's other partner, as if you could feel their feelings and think their thoughts. Imagine you are looking out through their eyes at your partner and at you, and notice what complicated bundle of emotions they are feeling about this situation, and how you and your parnter look to them, through their eyes. Then take three more deep breaths and imagine shifting back into your own shoes, and feeling your own feelings again.

4. Then imagine floating up above all three of you, seeing all three people, you, your partner, and their partner, and try to imagine that you could see all three points of view simultaneously.

After you complete this exercise, you may notice feeling more love for your partner and more understanding of their experience. Some people report feeling some compersion towards their partner because this exercise can help them grasp what their partner is feeling and gives them empathy for the both the pleasure and the pain that the partner is experiencing. And some people have felt compersion towards the outside partner because they can see that their position is far from secure or enviable.

An example: Zhang felt intense jealousy when her partner Thom slept overnight for the first time with Alicia, who he had been dating for a couple of months. She couldn't sleep, felt "crappy about myself for not being able to handle this," and felt betrayed and abandoned. In desperation she tried this exercise. In the first step, she felt more compassion for herself and realized her feelings were natural and that she needed to give herself credit for allowing Thom to spend the night with Alicia. As a result she felt proud of herself and felt strong rather than weak. In the second step, when she imagined being in her partner's shoes, she could see that he was caught in the middle and felt very stressed and anxious, since Alicia was demanding that he start spending the night with her, and Zhang was terribly frightened of it. She could see how hard he was trying to please both of them, and that this was being done only after carefully considering her feelings. During the third step, she tried to get inside Alicia's mind and understand her perspective, and she was shocked to feel some warmth and concern for Alicia. She realized that Alicia felt sad and mistreated when Thom would get up out of her bed and leave at midnight to go home. Zhang could easily imagine that this would feel awful to any woman, and felt compassion for Alicia lying in bed alone after Thom left. "That's similar to how I feel right now: lonely and hurt," she thought. She could see that all three of them were experiencing pain in this situation, and that everyone was making an effort to make this work. Before doing the exercise, she had felt victimized, that she was doing all the "work" and having all the pain while Thom and Alicia were getting all the benefits, and now she could see that this was not accurate.

Ambivalence between feelings of jealousy and compersion

Most of us have a long way to go before we will ever experience pure and unadulterated compersion. The best many of us can hope for is to feel less triggered with jealousy and closer to feeling neutral about our partner's outside sexual relationships. Some people have said that compersion is the opposite of jealousy, but my experience indicates otherwise. In fact, jealousy often co-exists with compersion. Many people go through a confusing combination of painful emotions that sometimes are mixed with some positive feelings, which they often find even more confusing!

Some examples:

In the midst of a jealousy melt-down, Adriana was vacillating wildly between two seemingly contradictory experiences. One day she was feeling completely crushed and betrayed by her husband Ruben starting a relationship with Jillian, a beautiful and brilliant scientist, and the next day she felt so proud of him and happy for his fabulous achievement! Jillian was gorgeous, affluent, and successful in her field. This made Adriana feel very threatened, as she felt Ruben might leave her for someone she felt was "superior" to her. At the same time she sincerely liked and admired Jillian, and was thrilled that her husband was able to command the respect and attraction of such an amazing woman, and this made her value him even more as a partner. And she knew that he had been socially awkward and had years of loneliness and feeling undesirable, so she was happy for him that he was experiencing such validation of his sexual desirablity. Because he was feeling so good, he began showering her with attention and gratitude, so she was on a roller-coaster between being angry at him and suspicious of Jillian's motives, and wanting to cheer Ruben on!

Kendra is a polyamorous married woman who had had several other sexual relationships during the ten years of her marriage. Her husband Jamal, a software developer, finally had his first relationship outside their marriage with Tasha, an engineer at his company. Kendra described simultaneous feelings of intense jealousy and compersion, which she found very perplexing. She was thrilled that he was finally reaping the benefits of their open marriage after many years of being monogamous by default, as he had difficulty finding women he felt comfortable with. However, since this was such a dramatic shift from how their marriage had always been, she was terrified that he would leave her for this new woman. Because Tasha was single and Jamal saw her every day at work, Kendra feared they would develop a strong bond that would threaten their marriage. "I was thrilled that he had found a wonderful woman who really made him feel safe enough to open up, but if she was so unique and special, she might replace me. I desperately wanted him to have this beautiful and deep love with her, but I was terrified it might come at the expense of our marriage." A fortunate coincidence helped ease her fears. While Tasha continued to have a relationship with Jamal, she fell in love with another man and married him. This allowed Kendra to finally feel more compersion, because Tasha's being married made her feel much safer.

While all of these reactions can be quite confusing and uncomfortable for most people, they are perfectly normal. Since you love your partner and want them to be happy, it is natural that you experience some positive feelings when you see them succeeding and enjoying something, even another love relationship! However, it is just as natural to feel threatened and anxious about your partner's romantic interest in someone else, so it makes sense that these seemingly contradictory feelings would co-exist. I advise my clients to expect a barrage of intense and confusing feelings, and accept whatever feelings come along without judging yourself! Many people only make things harder on themselves by telling themselves they "should" feel a certain way or that their feelings are "wrong." Take another wise woman's advice and stop "shoulding" all over yourself. Instead, practice compassion for yourself and your partner.

When compersion sneaks up on you

Sometimes compersion will sneak up on you when you least expect it.

Some examples:

Jimmie and Rebecca were on the verge of divorce because she was so jealous of him falling in love with Norma. Rebecca was convinced that Norma was out to steal her husband, and did everything to sabotage the relationship. Then Rebecca was diagnosed with breast cancer and had surgery, chemotherapy, and radiation treatments. During the nine months of her treatment, Norma cooked and delivered meals to their home, and went grocery shopping and ran errands for them. Rebecca began to feel more trusting and even fond of Norma, and grateful for her help.

Jimmie commuted to work during the day, and was in danger of losing his job if he took more time off to care for Rebecca. Norma was self-employed, so she was able to come over at lunchtime and make sure Rebecca got a hot meal and a shower every day. The two women bonded because they were spending a lot of time together without Jimmie, and Rebecca looked forward to seeing Norma every day. Rebecca said that in that in the bigger scheme of things, this relationship was not such a big deal compared to having cancer. And her husband's dedication to her throughout her illness convinced her that he was not going to leave her. After her recovery from the cancer, she gave her blessing to the their relationship.

Andi and Jinnie are a lesbian couple with two sons. Several months in couples counseling did not seem to help Jinnie accept Andi's outside relationship with Amanda. Jinnie complained that Andi went out for romantic dates with Amanda, while "I'm the boring wife at home and just do housework and take care of the kids." Amanda started to take the kids every other Saturday for an overnight, so Andi and Jinnie could have some romantic dates alone. At first they were actually uncomfortable without the kids there as a "buffer," and felt awkward having candlelight dinners and making out. Jinnie felt guilty for "abandoning the kids" and constantly called to make sure they were okay. But after a while, they started having a real sex life, for the first time since their pregnancies. And the two boys developed a great relationship with Amanda; she loved sports and took them to basketball games and out for pizza and movies. Jinnie was surprised when she began to feel compersion towards Andi's relationship with Amanda. She could see that the kids were both very attached to her and were getting a lot out of spending time with her. And she was grateful that Amanda was giving her the gift of time alone with Andi.

Compersion can go both ways

Sometimes compersion can go the other way. By this, I mean that the outside lover can experience intense jealousy and then eventually feel some compersion.

An example:

Marilyn and Raymond were a married couple in an open relationship. When Raymond got involved with Jeanne, she was extremely jealous of Marilyn's privileges as the wife, and railed against the unfairness of being "secondary." Marilyn empathized with Jeanne, and encouraged Raymond to spend more time with her, giving up some of her weekends so the two of them could go on romantic getaways. She coached Raymond to bring Jeanne flowers, buy her thoughtful gifts, and send her loving text messages and cards to show his commitment to her. While Raymond was clueless about romance, he was smart enough to take his wife's good advice, and slowly Jeanne began to feel more secure. Once she was getting enough of Raymond's time, loyalty, and respect as a partner, she felt more open to Marilyn and began emailing her and meeting her for coffee.

Chapter Seventeen:

Ask the jealousy experts – tips and techniques from professionals with expertise in jealousy in open relationships

Fortunately, many people have expertise on jealousy and open relationships. They have terrific advice to offer on this subject, and several of them were generous enough to contribute their best jealousy techniques to this book. Gathered in this chapter are a great collection of wisdom from a diverse array of brilliant people with many years of experience working with people in all types of open relationships. I encourage you to experiment with these techniques and discover which ones work best for you in different jealousy situations.

Exercise Thirty-five: Janet Hardy's "Jealousy As Teacher" Technique

Janet Hardy is an editor, publisher, and author of eleven books on subjects including polyamory, BDSM, spirituality, and sexual identity. She is co-author, with Dossie Easton, of <u>The Ethical Slut: A Practical Guide to Polyamory, Open Relationships & Other Adventures</u> (Random House, 2009), probably the most widely read book on polyamory. Her new memoir is <u>Girlfag: A Life Told In Sex and Musicals</u> (Beyond Binary Books, 2012). She lives, writes and cooks with her spouse, dogs, cat and chickens in Eugene, Oregon. She provided the following essay, deconstructing jealousy as an experience that has a lot to teach us about ourselves.

Step One: Remember that jealousy isn't fatal

Many myths surround polyamory, and some of the most pervasive and destructive have to do with jealousy.

The first, of course, is that jealousy is unsurvivable. (If I had a buck for every article I've read stating that "open relationships can never work; people get jealous," I could probably retire.) The second is that successful polyamorists never get jealous.

Well, I think I'm a pretty successful polyamorist, and I'm here to tell you: yes, I get jealous. I am perhaps less susceptible to jealousy than many people, but I've taken more than a few rides on that roller coaster, and I've lived to tell the tale.

In fact, I've learned to cherish my jealousy when it happens. I know that sounds a little masochistic – and I certainly have such tendencies – but it's more than that. It's that each round of jealousy I go through teaches me as much, if I let it, as a few dozen sessions in a therapist's office.

Step Two: Look at your fears and insecurities

Want to know what you're scared of? What you don't like about yourself? What traumas have scarred you, what assets you're proudest of? Start by taking inventory of your jealousy.

I began to notice this possibility during a previous long-term relationship with a heterosexual man. I discovered, somewhat to my own embarrassment, that I tended to feel more jealous when he slept with a woman who was younger or slimmer than me. Hey presto: Guess what I don't like about myself! Given that I don't see any practical way of getting younger, and that getting slimmer is more work than I feel like doing, I could either suffer with my jealousy, or work on loving those aspects of myself. I wish I could tell you that I have completely succeeded in either one, but I can report that my ability to love fat old me has improved considerably.

Step Three: Jealousy is negative emotion projected outward

In my experience, a good working definition of jealousy is "negative emotion projected outward." The jealous attack starts from whatever area is the sufferer's greatest weakness: in some people it might be ownership or territoriality, in others it might be the desire to be all things to their beloved, in yet others it might be feeling unworthy of love. (Those are three of the most common, but this is certainly not an exhaustive list.) When these feelings are projected onto the beloved, they become, in order: "She can't do that with someone else, she's *mine*"; "Why aren't I enough for him?"; "I'm terrified that she's going to fall in love with her girlfriend and leave me."

I suspect that jealousy has come, in the greater culture, to seem unsurvivable quite simply because *projecting negative emotion outward doesn't work*. If your lover stops seeing the girlfriend or boyfriend, that may temporarily assuage the turmoil you're feeling... but it cannot resolve the underlying problem of territoriality, codependency or feelings of unworthiness. No external person can possibly do that.

Step Four: Let jealousy point the way to the wound

Instead of projecting those negative emotions outward towards your partner or their other relationships, I propose the radical step of letting jealousy point the way to the wound. When jealousy attacks, you can take it as a signpost of an aspect of yourself that requires healing, and get to work – on your own or with the help of a trusted friend or therapist – on healing it.

I don't want to make it sound, here, like this process will lead to becoming a paragon of security and self-love who will never again experience a flutter of jealousy. It won't. That's not the nature of healing – perhaps because humans don't live long enough to do that much work, or perhaps because a wound always leaves a scar. You will always have moments when the old, bad feeling wants to creep back, and you may always experience some jealous feelings.

But the more you practice this habit of looking inward instead of outward for a solution to your jealousy, the easier, I've found, it becomes. With time, motivation and self-love, you can learn to survive jealousy, and become a stronger and happier person in the process.

Exercise Thirty-six: Wendy-O Matik's "Self-Compassion Meditation for Jealousy"

Wendy-O Matik has been called a "polyamory advocate and radical love warrior." She is a poet, publisher, and author of <u>Redefining Our Relationships: Guidelines for Responsible Open Relationships,</u> a feminist critique of love and relationships outside the dominant paradigm of monogamy. Her website, www.wendyomatik. com, is a great resource for anyone considering open relationships. For the past decade she has been teaching "The Radical Love & Relationship Workshops" internationally, helping to shape alternative relationship models for the 21st century. As an educator and spokesperson for the polyamory community, Wendy has become an activist of the heart who pushes the boundaries of society's notions of relationships, love, gender, sexual equality, and sexual politics. She defines "radical love as the freedom to love whom you want, how you want, as many as you want, so long as personal integrity, respect, honesty, and consent are at the core of all relationships." Her workshops primarily focus on love and intimacy rather than sex and sexual conquest. Wendy shared this meditation as a tool for managing jealousy, based on mindfulness meditation techniques.

When you are in the painful throes of jealousy, your mind and body riddled with fear, insecurity, and anxiety, there is a tendency to shut down, pull away and blame. Jealousy can be so intense that you may contemplate breaking up, moving out, or leaving the country altogether. Mindfulness meditation is an effective technique for deepening and enriching your intimate relationships. Since it takes practice to stay deeply connected and truly intimate with loved ones, a daily meditation practice is helpful for fostering gratitude, trust, empathy, and loving-kindness.

The following exercise has the power to initiate change – change in your relationship to yourself, in your ideas about how you live and interact with others, in how you experience your jealousy, in order to allow you to find new meaning and purpose in your life beyond your jealousy. Despite how upsetting and unsettling it is when jealousy rears its scary head in your life, it is a time for offering deep compassion and tenderness to yourself. Take this mindful moment to do just that, step by step, breath by breath.

Step One: Find a place to sit and relax

To become fully aware of the present moment, simply follow your breathing. Take a conscious breath, noticing your inhale and your exhale. Notice the cool air filling your nose on the inhale and the release of warm air leaving your lungs on the exhale. Try this for a few breaths.

Step Two: Set your intentions for your practice

Say aloud or to yourself, "May this exercise deepen my self-compassion and allow me to experience my thoughts and feelings without judgment. May this meditation open my heart to the understanding and the tenderness that I need." You may want to make your intention more specific, such as "May this relaxing experience reduce my insecurities and soften my jealous anger," or "Let this practice help me stay open to my partner and let go of a desire to control the future."

Step Three: Focus on your physical sensations of jealousy

Begin to peel back the layers of jealousy and sort through your physical experience. Where do you experience jealousy in your body? You may be feeling knots in your stomach, tension in your neck and shoulders, or a burning sensation on your skin and face. Notice where jealousy flares up for you in a physical way. Pay attention to the different and varying shifts of these sensations. Whenever you start to feel your mind wander, focus on your breathing, become aware of the sound and the rhythm of your breath, and reconnect with the present moment.

Step Four: Notice the feelings and emotions of jealousy

Take this time to pause and reflect on your feelings of jealousy. What emotions are stirring inside you, alongside the jealousy? Are you angry, or simply disappointed? Do you feel abandoned or left out of plans? Maybe you had a stressful day at work and, in addition to the jealousy, you feel overwhelmed, disconnected, and exhausted. Sit with these emotions and observe their migration. Some emotions may feel more prominent and others less so. Simply take note of what comes up emotionally for you without attaching a story or explanation for it. If you catch yourself placing a judgment on your emotions or labeling your feelings good or bad, fair or unfair, right or wrong, take a moment to remind yourself that emotions are just emotions, neither good nor bad. Focus on just the actual feelings and keep breathing.

Step Five: Identify your jealous thoughts

The last layer for reflection is your jealous thoughts. Take this mindful moment to pay attention to what comes up for you mentally when you are jealous. You may have splices of a recent conversation broiling in your mind. You may be creating new scripts for what you'll say later to your partner(s) or lover(s). You may have a spiraling of questions encircling your mind.

Step Six: Notice any shifts in sensations, feelings, and thoughts

Start to notice how thoughts, feelings and sensations come and go, shift and change, ebb and flow. Your experience of jealousy in your mind, body and heart are momentary, passing, and impermanent. Everything is shifting and changing.

Step Seven: Check in with yourself

Take a few more conscious breaths, fully aware of this present moment unfolding into the next present moment, and move gently with yourself, offer tenderness and compassion at every step. Check in with how you're feeling now. As you connect more deeply with yourself, you will be able to have more capacity to connect more deeply with others.

This mindful exercise is an extremely useful tool in helping you cope with jealousy. It can help you become aware of the complex layers of physical sensations, feelings, and thoughts that can create a painful and confusing stew of jealousy. When you feel trapped by jealous thoughts, feelings and sensations, a daily mindfulness practice will deepen your empathy and soften your reaction to your jealousy. You don't have to spend hours meditating – just a few minutes each day can help shift your perspective on the situation that is sparking your jealousy, and give you greater understanding and compassion for yourself and your partner.

Exercise Thirty-seven: Dawn Davidson's "Juggling for Idiots" Jealousy Tapping Exercise

Dawn Davidson is a Certified Interchange Radical Counselor and a Certified Shamanic Soul Coach. Dawn is passionate about helping relationship explorers to experience greater fulfillment in their lives and loves. Her website, www.LoveOutsideTheBox.com, is overflowing with great tips for successful open relationships, including managing jealousy. As a coach and presenter, she provides insightful, intuitive guidance, along with wide-ranging experience and resources. She has a book coming out this year called <u>KISSable Agreements</u>, a guide for creating open relationship agreements. She suggests this quick and powerful jealousy technique, humorously titled "Juggling for Idiots."

In 1987, Francine Shapiro discovered that eye movements across the midline of the face could be helpful in reducing her own emotional charge around negative events. She went on to create Eye Movement, Desensitization and Reprocessing, known as EMDR, a powerful technique that has been proven useful in treating many serious challenges, including PTSD. While EMDR is generally done by a trained therapist, there is a simple way you can use a variation of it on yourself. The goal is to reduce the emotional intensity and pain triggered by jealousy, helping you assess the situation in a more rational frame of mind and respond more calmly.

Step One: Sit comfortably and close your eyes. Cross your arms over your chest, comfortably resting one hand on each shoulder.

Step Two: Create a sense of being in the triggering event, the specitic situation that made you feel jealous. This can be done in two parts: First, imagine a "freeze frame" of the recent moment you started feeling the jealousy, just like a photo of that moment. Then, remember a "self-referential statement," a feeling or thought you had at that moment of jealousy (e.g., "I will be all alone," "I am powerless," "My partner doesn't love me"). Recreate the physical and emotional sensations as much as possible. This can feel alarming – that's a normal response, and it is necessary to resolve this situation. It is very important to hold onto this combination of feeling and remembering while doing the exercise. You may have multiple triggering events. If so, start with one, and repeat the exercise for other jealousy triggers if you choose.

Step Three: Begin alternately tapping the fronts of your shoulders with the right and left hands. Continue this tapping as long as you choose to. Notice how your feelings change as you continue tapping – it is likely that the feelings will ebb and flow and shift over time as you tap.

Optional: To increase efficacy, do this at a slow enough pace so that you can move your eyes back and forth as well, "looking" at each hand as you tap and holding the scene and feelings in your mind (this can be done with the eyes closed).

Step Four: As you continue tapping, it may become harder to stay present in the feelings, and that is natural. You may experience a sense of confusion, and that's also OK. Just hold onto the scene as best you can for as long as you can. Keep noticing how the feelings about it change.

This exercise is very useful during an acute jealousy episode, as it usually will quickly reduce the intensity of the painful emotions, and allow you to become more clear-headed and able to function.

Exercise Thirty-eight: Francesca Gentille's "Technique for When Your Partner Is Triggered"

Francesca Gentille is a teacher, writer, and shaman. She explains that your partner can become "triggered" by words, behaviors, facial expressions, being in specific environments, even by smells or tastes. These triggers have a meaning for that person, usually due to past trauma from childhood or a past relationship. This experience reminds them of that past situation and "triggers" them into a distressed state where they are much less resilient and resourceful in managing their feelings. While someone can be triggered in many different kinds of situations, triggers frequently happen in response to something happening in a polyamorous relationship, causing intense jealousy. She suggests the following sequence to show love and compassion for your partner to help them through, while they are in a non-resourceful state. Her website is at www. integrativeartsinstitute.com.

In life, love, or in processing an interaction, a person can suddenly be triggered into a trauma state.

Step One: Look for the signs and symptoms

Signs of being triggered are:

- Not being able to look at you

- A marked difference in tone, breathing, rapidity of speech, body posture

- Stuttering, if they do not usually stutter

- Sounding significantly younger, or like someone else entirely

- Swearing profusely when they rarely if ever swear

- Rubbing of the forehead, neck, arms, hands

- Suddenly falling asleep

- Not being able to talk at all

Many different terms are used to describe this state, such as

- Fight

- Flight

- Freeze

- Dissocation

- Flipping/switching into another Inner Aspect/Self/Persona/Age/Alter

Something you have inadvertently said or done has unconsciously awakened a similarity to a painful experience in the past, and they are reacting by using the survival strategies that helped them survive that past event.

Step Two: Look inside yourself to manage your own reactions first, before approaching your partner

When the thought goes through your mind, "I wonder if they are triggered"...

1. Slow down

2. Lengthen your breathing

3. Feel your feet on the earth

4. Release judgment of yourself and this person

5. See the suffering underneath their actions

6. Breathe into compassion for yourself and them

7. Become quiet

8. Ground and center yourself before speaking

Step Three: Make an educated guess about how your partner may be feeling

9. Try to imagine being in your partner's shoes right now. Gently and tenderly, make your best guess, from the *first person*, about what they may be feeling right now, and ask them to correct you if you have guessed wrong. For example, you might say, "If I were sitting with my hands rubbing my forehead and my eyes looking down, as you are right now, it would mean that I felt scared. Perhaps little. Is that at all like what you are feeling?

10. Breathe and wait patiently for your partner to find an ability to speak.

11. If the person attacks with something like: "Duh!" "It's because of what *you* said!" "You're not a very good boyfriend/girlfriend," etcetera... *breathe.* Practice compassion for yourself and then them (silently). Remember that this big response is not about you. Let it flow down to the ground and out of your body.

12. Appreciate them for doing their best to protect themselves. (Mean it.) Appreciate – appreciate – appreciate.

13. Don't take anything personally. Don't take anything personally. Don't take anything personally.

The Jealousy Workbook

Step Four: Provide silent empathy

14. Hold compassionate space in your heart. Silently, brainstorm how they might be feeling right now, or what might have happened in the past that would have them so scared and angry now. You are entering what Marshall Rosenberg calls "Silent Empathy." It is a field of energy that the person will begin to feel, but that energy may take a while to start sinking in. Don't give up before it has time to take hold!

Step Five: If no shift occurs, provide these additional supports

15. Get them some food and something to drink, and offer it to them or put it near them. Don't force it upon them.

16. Offer to leave the room for a short time and return, if they would like a little space and solitude. Let them know you are going to get centered and will be right back. Don't expect them to answer, depending on how triggered they are.

17. Gently slow down and lengthen your breathing. In a very neutral tone, invite them to do the same. You are in a mirrored field. If you doubt, become anxious, shut down or judge, they will feel even less safe. You are the Dominant Limbic System Center yourself; gently guide with heart.

Exercise Thirty-nine: Terry Brussel's "Joy without Jealousy" Self-Hypnosis Technique

Dr. Terry Brussels is a hypnotherapist in Southern California who has been working with people in open relationships for over forty years. She is Director of the Success Center (www.acesuccess.com) and has developed a series of guided imagery CDs and audio downloads entitled "Intimacy Without Jealousy," designed to help manage and reduce jealousy. These focus on enhancing self-esteem, calming anxiety, and addressing insecurities which contribute to creating jealousy. The following exercise is taken from one of her audio downloads, "Joy Without Jealousy."

(Note: If you do not swim or have any fears of swimming or water, do not utilize this particular exercise, as it involves images of swimming and water. Many of Dr. Brussel's other downloads will be more appropriate for you.)

Step One: Relax through deep breathing and progressive muscle relaxation

Get into a comfortable position, close your eyes, and relax through taking some deep breaths. Then, slowly relax your entire body through progressive muscle relaxation. You can do this by first relaxing your feet, then taking another breath to relax your legs, then another breath and relax your hips, then your back, then your shoulders, your arms and hands, your neck, your face and head.

Step Two: Set your intention and practice positive affirmations

Remind yourself that your intention is to relieve yourself of the anxieties and insecurities that are creating and feeding your jealousy. Set a goal of imagining yourself as strong, confident, relaxed, and able to accept your partner having other relationships. Visualize an image in your mind of yourself becoming calm, loving, and welcoming of your partner's other partner. Say these affirmation to yourself silently,

1. More and more, every day, I am becoming the person I wish to be.

2. I love myself, and I love my partner.

3. I feel safe and secure in my relationship.

4. I know my partner loves and values me.

5. I feel better and better about myself every day.

6. I feel more loved and secure about my relationship with each day that goes by.

Step Three: Swimming across the lake

Imagine yourself swimming easily and effortlessly across a beautiful lake on a spectacular summer day. With every stroke, you are feeling stronger, more confident, and you are safe and energized. You are swimming slowly, breathing deeply, feeling the strength in your body as you get closer to the other side of the lake, leaving more and more of your jealousy and possessiveness behind as you see the shore coming closer with every breath. As you reach the shore on the other side of the lake, you notice how good you are feeling, and how much you have achieved. You feel much more accepting of your partner, and of all your partner's other friendships, including their platonic friends, their family members, and their other lovers. Repeat to yourself this affirmation: "I feel more and more accepting and welcoming of my partner's other relationships."

Step Four: Remember that you can make choices

Remind yourself that at all times, you are in control of your own choices. You can choose to focus on your own inner security, which comes from within you, rather than from any external source. You can empower yourself to feel safe, rather than giving others power over your feeling of security.

Step Five: Nurture compersion

Through utilizing this exercise and these affirmations, you can eventually accept and welcome your partner's other relationship. Try to imagine yourself feeling "compersion," a feeling of being happy for your partner that they are receiving love from another partner. Visualize yourself sharing in your partner's joy in experiencing more love, and seeing how your partner's happiness enriches your life and your relationship.

Chapter Nineteen:

Buddhist jealousy advice from an atheist

"Thousands of candles can be lit from a single candle and the life of that candle will not be shortened. Happiness never decreases by being shared." (attributed to the Buddha)

You might wonder why an atheist like me would be offering Buddhist advice on jealousy. The answer is that I once randomly stumbled across some practical help from the Buddha himself while in the midst of a jealousy attack. Further investigation revealed some Buddhist concepts and techniques which many of my clients have found useful in "turning down the volume" on jealousy episodes. You may find some of these Buddhist techniques helpful regardless of your religious persuasion (or lack thereof).

You may be aware of a Buddhist concept which is sometimes described as "non-attachment." While countless volumes have been written on this concept, the Cliff's Notes version is this: The more attached you become to any person, object, experience, or future outcome, the more you try to possess it, and the more pain you can cause yourself and others through your fear of losing it. The Buddha's advice: try to loosen your grip a little on whatever (and whomever) you are trying to possess and control. Becoming less attached to having and keeping everything you want in life allows you to feel more satisfied with what you have and less focused on possibly losing it. This helps you accept that you do not control the universe or other people. (My apologies to any real Buddhists for this oversimplification of a very complex concept, but my purpose is not theological discourse but rather to explain how this concept may be helpful for jealousy.)

Exercise Forty: Shift from attachment to connection

How can this concept of "non-attachment" help you? We have been taught by our culture that our partner belongs to us, and that we are entitled to their love as if it is an object that could be possessed. Some of you may recall folksinger Teresa Trull's song lyrics, "I don't have relationships, I take hostages." While most of us do not want to keep our partners in "love jail," some people think that non-attachment sounds like we don't care about the relationship. It is healthy to develop attachments to people we love and who are important in our lives, our partner as well as family members and friends. However, our compulsive need to control our partner can become excessive. So I prefer to re-frame this concept as shifting away from a clinging and possessive mode of attachment and instead moving towards connection. This process can help you feel very connected with your partner and aware of how precious your relationship is to you, while not holding your partner hostage with your fear of loss.

Step One: Imagine what attachment looks like

Start by closing your eyes for a moment and trying to visualize what your attachment to your partner looks like when you are feeling jealous, as if you could see a picture of it in your mind's eye. If you are artistically inclined, you may get more benefit out of this exercise by actually drawing or painting a picture of it yourself. This step may be unpleasant because jealousy makes most of us feel very needy and possessive, and we would rather not see ourselves as so dependent and vulnerable.

A few examples:

Rita explained that when she imagined her attachment in her current state of jealousy, she saw an image of her partner Maxwell behind a locked door, with herself guarding the door.

Martin imagined himself grabbing his partner George's legs while George was trying to run away.

Leo drew a picture of his wife Mary as a graceful willow tree and himself as a passion flower vine wrapping itself all around the branches of the tree.

Lisa was shocked that when she thought of her attachment to Erica, she saw them holding hands and gazing into each other's eyes and they both were pleading out loud, "Please love me! Please love me!"

Jim drew a picture of himself scowling as he repeatedly texted his lover Roxanne with interrogating questions and requests for reassurance, and she frantically sent him texts back, with a thick black line connecting his phone to hers.

Step Two: What would connection look like?

When you are jealous, the expression of your attachment is likely to be focused on controlling your partner in order to stabilize your relationship. Buddhist teachings describe attachment as being too dependent on something outside of yourself for your happiness, whether that is a relationship, a possession, a substance such as drugs or alcohol, wealth, status, or even an experience. Rather than striving to secure and possess any or all of the above, Buddha suggested accepting that all these are impermanent, and seeking inner peace instead through letting go of our attachment to having them. Since they are fleeting, we cannot possess them, and ultimately they cannot bring us happiness.

What I believe is useful about this theory is that if we loosen the Vulcan Death Grip of our attachment to our partner, we can move towards a healthier and more satisfying experience of connection. Connection with our partner means that we see our relationship as a special gift which we feel privileged to experience, rather than seeing it as our possession to be controlled and guarded. This way of experiencing relationship is likely to reduce your jealousy. Take a moment and try to imagine what connection would look like in your relationship if you could magically create it, or draw a picture of how you would imagine it. How is it different than your picture of attachment in Step One?

A few examples:

Rita tried to move from attachment to connection by changing the image of Maxwell behind a locked door with her as his prison guard. She imagined instead that they were sitting together at the kitchen table and feeding each other strawberries dipped in chocolate, and telling each other about their respective dates with other partners the night before.

Martin changed the image of him holding onto George's legs, to an image of them jogging together in a ten-mile race to raise money for cancer research.

Leo felt the image of Mary as the willow tree was fine, but instead of seeing himself as a clinging vine, he imagined himself as bunches of flowers growing near the base of the tree.

Lisa felt the image of she and Erica holding hands symbolized connection, but changed the dialogue to each of them saying "I love you very much, and I support you having other lovers."

Jim changed the image from constant anxious texts back and forth to Roxanne, to a short text in the morning and the evening, and a phone call on his lunch hour to check in about the amusing events of the day, and making plans for a special date night each week.

Learn something from the Buddhist lesbians

The late Celeste West was a Buddhist scholar, librarian, and author of a diverse array of books ranging from *Revolting Librarians* to *Zen in a Nutshell* to The *Lesbian Love Advisor*. Her most controversial book, *Lesbian Polyfidelity: A Pleasure Guide for all Women whose Hearts are Open to Multiple Sexualoves*, seamlessly combines Buddhist teachings with open relationships and includes seven chapters on jealousy. She describes herself as a a "former raving jealousoid," and her advice is useful not only for lesbians and Buddhists, but everyone else as well.

This brief summary cannot do justice to her wonderfully complex program for defusing and reducing jealousy. However, I present a few nuggets here, and highly recommend that you read her book to receive the maximum benefit of her wisdom.

Step One: Relax through meditation, relaxation techniques, and deep breathing

West notes that most people experience intense anxiety as either a primary symptom or side effect of jealousy, so she believes that relaxation training is an essential tool "to quiet the squirrel cage" of jealousy. Unsurprisingly, as a Buddhist teacher, she recommends meditation and deep breathing techniques. Any method of relaxation, whether Buddhist or not, will help you consciously slow down, get a grip on your fears, and become more comfortable with whatever is provoking your jealousy. Many relaxation methods are based on "mindfulness," a somewhat vague term that generally includes a focus on slow, deep breathing and consciously emptying your mind of stressful thoughts, staying in the present moment as much as possible. West reminds us that "anxiety is just excitement without breathing," so her advice is to keep breathing and try to get some distance from your knee-jerk reactions to see the full picture and feel more grounded and in control.

Step Two: Get enough sleep, by any means necessary, to stay sane through the jealousy experience

Most people have a very hard time sleeping when their partner is out on a date with someone else. Lying awake half the night obsessing about what your partner is doing with someone else can literally make some people suicidal. This insomnia is usually caused by a potent mix of facing two very unfamiliar experiences at the same time. Most couples are used to sleeping together in the same bed every night, and suddenly you are all alone in the bed and possibly alone in the house. And your partner is not just off on a business trip, but is out with another lover, so that additional new twist is extremely disconcerting and can keep you up all night. In the morning you are exhausted, depressed, and angry: not the ideal state of mind (or body) to manage your jealousy or greet your partner when they waltz in high on sex and infatuation. This situation creates a non-resourceful state where even the most well-adjusted polyamorist will feel overwhelmed and unable to cope.

The Jealousy Workbook

West wisely points out the importance of treating jealousy-induced insomnia with herbal sleeping remedies or other medications or methods to make sure you get a good night's sleep. She suggests that you be out on a date with someone else on the same nights your partner is seeing someone else – mutual "date nights" each week, so you will be distracted and not thinking about your partner's date, and hopefully you will sleep better after some rousing sex with someone else.

Step Three: Focus on your relationship and work to improve it; don't focus on your partner's outside relationships

West points out that many people spend a lot of energy focused on their partner's other relationships, and devote too much precious time in their own relationship processing the outside relationships and negotiating demands about them. She believes this is counterproductive and actually futile, as your goal should be improving your own relationship rather than policing any other relationship. Instead, she suggests a two-pronged approach towards deepening your primary relationship: 1) shower your partner with love, attention, and affection, and 2) ask directly for whatever you want in your relationship. Since you can only actually control yourself and your own relationship, any attempts to control the other relationship will only make it more attractive, and are doomed to failure.

She suggests that at the beginning of any new outside relationship, you set these minimum standards for your partner, and ask them to agree to them, preferably in writing.

1. Set fun, intimate time at least once a week.

2. Honor all economic and public commitments.

3. Agree to perform all the usual chores.

4. Call for a wide berth between the primary partner and the new lover, for the present.

West says that if your partner cannot meet these standards of participation in your relationship while in the midst of a new crush, they are not ready for an open relationship, because they clearly are not capable or keeping their prior commitments while adding on something new.

Step Four: Journal about your jealousy

She says, "Like the rest of us, when she is organized, jealousy is more productive. Use what is left of your mind to list all the paranoid speculations and imaginings which now regale your love life." First write out all your fears, resentments, and everything you are feeling, and all the alleged misdeeds of your partner or their other partner. She suggests running these by a trusted friend to see how close to reality you are, and that just saying them out loud to another person will help you put them into perspective. A particularly humorous fear she had was "She will use the recipes I created for a seduction dinner for XX." She then suggests a ritual for burning those pages, as a symbolic way of letting go of your jealousy as much as possible.

Step Five: Pursue your own meaningful activities

While your first impulse may be to focus on your jealousy and whatever situation has provoked it, West suggests instead using this opportunity to pursue activities that give you pleasure, satisfaction, and meaning. Channel the energy you were about to spend obsessing in a jealous fit into planning a fabulous trip, doing gardening, taking a dance class, starting some volunteer work, going out with friends – anything nurturing and stimulating that recharges your batteries.

She explains, "It does not work to treat jealousy as an unruly employee, either to be disciplined or dismissed." She reminds us that the word jealousy comes from the Greek word *zelos*, which means "zeal," and suggests putting that zeal into something more fun and productive. She especially recommends activities that require some physical exercise, since exercise gets the anxiety and anger out of your system.

Step Six: Confront the other partner if they behave badly

You may be surprised that West suggests confronting your partner's other partner if they are trying to sabotage your relationship. This may sound territorial and un-Buddhist, but she suggests talking with the other partner if they are asking your partner to break relationship agreements or are pushing to displace you as the primary partner. Her advice is to politely but firmly explain that you welcome this new relationship and will treat this new person with respect, but that you expect the same in return. She believes this will help clear up any misunderstandings about your relationship agreements, and will scare off anyone whose goal is to break up your relationship and walk away with your partner.

Step Seven: Remember that there are worse things than your fears

Tragically, two of West's lovers died over a short period of time, one of cancer and the other of natural causes. After all the jealousy episodes where she was terrified of losing them to another lover, she was stunned that instead it was death that took them from her. "I thus came to measure all loss in terms of the ultimate." Suddenly jealousy seemed absurd, and time with her lovers became too precious to waste on jealous drama.

This reminded me of a Buddhist parable in which a monk describes a ceramic cup he uses each morning for his tea, saying that he loves the cup because it is already broken. When his student points out that the cup is not broken, he replies that he knows that the cup will someday break, so he has already accepted that he will lose this cup eventually. And knowing that makes him appreciate the cup even more, and enjoy every moment that he has the cup even more because of its impermanent nature.

The reality is that someday you and your partner will be separated, either by one partner's death or by breaking up. While we would prefer to avoid thinking about either death or divorce, one or the other will claim your relationship eventually. This sobering reality check may help you put your jealousy in perspective, and allow you to experience that shift from attachment to connection.

The straight white men have something useful to say about it, too

Dr Mark Epstein is a Buddhist psychiatrist who has written several books on the Buddha's teachings. In his book *Open to Desire,* Epstein radically reexamines the Buddha's approach to desire, sexual and otherwise. He suggests that it is not desire itself, but rather the clinging and craving that seem to go along with desire, that cause most of human suffering. He describes the seeming paradox that when you fall in love you are yearning for total union with the beloved. However, that attempt at merging is doomed to failure because you will always remain two separate people. The reality cannot live up to these unrealistic expectations of bliss, leading to a feeling of disappointment and longing.

Attempts to cling to your partner are fueled by a craving that cannot be completely satisfied by a partner, as it is unrealistic to project all of your unmet needs onto them. Epstein advises that while the desire for love, connection, and sexual satisfaction are all perfectly normal, carried to unhealthy extremes they will lead to unhappiness. Looking to your partner for fulfillment is a way of avoiding yourself and the existential responsibility for your own happiness. Instead, he suggests that a love relationship should be "a place of co-creation and mutual recognition."

In a jealousy crisis, there is a tendency to become much more clinging, demanding more time, attention, and affirmation from your partner. At a time like this, it may seem natural to become more possessive rather than trying to take care of yourself. Epstein says that in Buddhist thought, "masculine energy is associated with possession, acquisition, and objectification," where "the self actively tries to get its needs met by manipulating its environment." He suggests instead a strategy of developing a stronger sense of yourself independently from your partner. A Japanese Buddhist principle called *miegakure,* or "hide and reveal," is illustrated in Japanese gardens, where a meandering waterfall comes in and out of the line of vision as you walk along a path. Allowing your partner to move in and out of your presence, through their spending time with another partner, allows you both to be stronger as individuals, yet feel secure in your connection. Like the waterfall, your partner will return to you again and again as you continue on your path.

Chapter Nineteen:

Using Neuro-linguistic Programming (NLP™) to experience more "Emotional Choice"

Most people feel overwhelmed and out of control when jealousy or any other strong emotion occurs. We believe that we have no control over our emotions – that they appear unbidden, making us helpless victims. In the grip of a jealousy attack, most of us feel powerless, as if we have been thrown down into a pit of pain with no way to climb out.

To create a powerful tool for a jealousy crisis, I have adapted two of Leslie Lebeau's "Emotional Choice" techniques. Ms. Lebeau (previously known as Leslie Cameron-Bandler) has taught Neuro-linguistic Programming (NLP) for nearly forty years, and developed many of the most powerful techniques of this modality. To grossly oversimplify a huge and complex subject, NLP is a cognitive behavioral therapy which dissects thoughts, feelings, and behaviors in order to help people understand themselves and others better. Through changing the way people think, behave, and communicate, NLP techniques strive to create competence and successful outcomes in interpersonal relationships as well as in work situations. While these techniques were not developed for jealousy or for open

relationships, they can be extremely helpful in developing a greater feeling of control over your jealousy and having access to more positive emotions even during a jealousy experience. These techniques originated in her book, *The Emotional Hostage,* and I have modified each one specifically for jealousy.

Special nerd alert: Some people have suggested that NLP techniques are most useful for people who are highly intellectual or are mechanically minded. No technical knowledge is needed to do these exercises, but I have noticed that engineers, scientists, computer professionals, and accountants get very excited about these techniques. One math professor reported that they were much more helpful in understanding and managing his jealousy than "all that other touchy-feely hippie stuff you gave me." An chemistry researcher said she "really enjoyed geeking out on my jealousy with those NLP exercises!" If you are a Luddite, don't hesitate to try these exercises, as they may be very useful to you. However, I would like to extend a special invitation to the left-brain crowd to try these out as they have been, as one client put it, "nerd beta-tested."

Exercise Forty-one: Identify and modify the components of your emotional experience

Identify the instruments in the jealousy orchestra

Lebeau describes any intense emotion as a symphony orchestra. When you feel trapped in an emotion's powerful grip, it is like hearing Beethoven's *Fifth* as one big sound, but not being able to pick out the sounds of the drums, the trumpets, the violins, etc. Identifying the "instruments" or components can help you understand and establish more control over your emotional experience. She identifies the following pieces of the puzzle:

- The time frame

- The modality

- Involvement

- Intensity

- Comparison

- Tempo

- Criteria

- Chunk size

Step One: Clarify the time frame

This step refers to whether the current emotional state is focused on the past, present, or future, and whether your emotional reaction will generate the best outcomes for both the present and the future. For instance, feeling regret, guilt, or depression is almost always about something that happened in the past; feeling restless, bored, or stuck is about something that is happening in the present; feeling anxious or frightened is worrying about something that will happen sometime in the future. Identifying the time frame of an emotion can be helpful in assessing its usefulness and in modifying it.

When you feel jealous, try to identify whether your feelings are about the present situation, or whether they are based in the past or the future. Try to center your emotions in the present moment, and then make your best effort to respond and behave in a way that will create the best outcome for yourself and for your relationship.

A few examples:

Teresa was very angry when her husband Jonas went on a date with a new woman, and when he returned late that night she screamed at him and accused him of betraying her. In hindsight, she realized that in the present time frame she was furious, but that this emotional response only generated behavior that would sabotage her marriage for the future. As a result, the next time, she was able to express her anger by writing it all out in her journal, and thinking about the future effect it would have if she yelled at him again, and she felt much calmer. When he came home, she was able to honestly tell him that she had experienced some anger but that it had dissipated, and now she just needed to be held and reassured.

Anthony became quite depressed when his partner Jane developed a sexual relationship with a colleague that she met at a conference. He realized that his sadness was based on his past experience of being abandoned by his former wife, who divorced him after developing a relationship with her boss. Understanding that his pain was based on the past allowed him to bring his attention to the present time frame and remind him that Jane was trustworthy and would not leave him.

Julia and her wife Samantha are both midwives in private practice together, and Julia also has a relationship with Fran. Julia was slow-dancing at a club with Fran and ran into one of their patients. When Samantha heard about it, she became extremely jealous because she feared that their patients might start gossiping about them. She realized that her fears were about being publicly humiliated in the future, and in bringing her concerns back into the present, her jealousy was reduced.

Step Two: Shift to a more positive modality

Modality is your attitude or beliefs about three things: the importance or necessity of achieving something, your responsibility for doing it, and the actual possibility of successfully doing so. You can reduce your emotional distress in any jealousy situation by repeating these three affirmations:

"It is necessary to manage this,"

"I am the only person that can do this task," and

"It is possible for me to do this."

A jealousy attack can make you feel helpless and stuck. Deciding that it is necessary to do something about it helps you change from a passive stance of avoidance and anxiety into action mode. Realizing that the task is yours and only yours to do moves you from feeling like a victim, dependent on your partner to fix it, to being more in control of your life. Telling yourself that it is possible to manage your jealousy in this particular situation empowers you to feel more confident and competent. This won't be an instant transformation, but rather a way of shifting your emotional experience from helplessness to feeling that you can actually handle this, as difficult as it may be.

Step Three: Create active involvement

The next step is actively creating the outcome you desire. "Involvement" means setting a goal for changing your jealous distress to a more comfortable or positive emotional experience, and then taking at least one active step towards that end. Most people experience jealousy as an agonizing state of paralysis, and one sure way of lessening that hopeless feeling is to take *some* action, even if you are not sure what to do.

Start by noticing which feeling is most intolerable, and set your intention of moving away from that feeling and toward whatever feeling seems like its opposite. For instance, if you feel crushed with sadness and loneliness because your lover is spending the day with another partner, imagine moving away from those feelings and toward joy and companionship. Then brainstorm at least one action that might create that reality. You might decide to watch Comedy Central for an hour to laugh and feel amused, or you might phone a friend for a long chat, or take the dog to the dog park to be around people and feel more connected. Your jealousy is unlikely to vanish, but you are likely to feel better, and through practice, and some trial and error, you will discover what actions will give you the most relief.

Step Four: Lower or contain the intensity

Emotions have differing levels of intensity, which can make any experience, including jealousy, easier or harder to handle. For instance, there is a continuum from mild annoyance, to irritation, to frustration, to anger, to rage – from the least intense to the most intolerably intense feeling. In any jealousy situation, you will be better able to cope if you are able to lower the intensity of the emotions you are feeling, or if you can notice the feeling when it is still at a lower intensity, and contain it before it escalates to a more intense emotion.

A few examples:

Rajee reported becoming "frantic with out-of-control terror" when her partner Dean told her he was developing stronger feelings for his other lover Kelly. She hoped to prevent a repeat performance during a planned processing discussion the next evening. I asked Rajee to try to notice when she started to feel anxious, and see if she could keep the emotion from changing to a more intensely negative feeling. She remembered when Dean disclosed these feelings for Kelly, the first thing she noticed was "feeling a little concerned," which rapidly turned into anxiety, then morphed into feeling very agitated and upset, and soon became what she described as "terrified hysteria." So the next night during their talk, as soon as she felt "concerned," she took some deep breaths and made a conscious effort to stay at that level of intensity. Despite her best efforts, she felt the feelings escalating from concern to mild and then moderate anxiety, but was able to stay at that level until the end of the conversation, when it subsided altogether. With a little more practice in subsequent scary jealousy situations, she became more competent at keeping the distress to a minimum, and preventing uncomfortable emotions from becoming more intense.

Annie was crushed when her partner Elsa admitted that she had brought her girlfriend Nan to their home and had sex in their bed while Annie was at work. While they had not had an explicit prohibition on this, Elsa said she knew it would be very painful for Annie. She apologized for "just getting carried away," and promised never to do it again. Annie felt such despair that she had trouble breathing and felt like she would throw up. She knew if she could lower the intensity she could move through this terrible pain. She asked Elsa to hold her and stroke her hair, and she reminded herself that Elsa had just made a mistake and she trusted her to do better next time. Slowly she felt the knot in her stomach start to loosen up, and her despair softened into feeling sad but calmer and more hopeful. She described the experience as "shifting from a 10 on the sadness scale to about a 6, which still sucked but was much more tolerable."

Step Five: Stop making comparisons

This refers to the unfortunate human tendency to compare ourselves to other people, and usually to find ourselves coming up short. A jealousy attack only amplifies our compulsion to see how we measure up against the competition. And because our self-esteem is usually at an all-time low when we feel intensely jealous, we are bound to feel inadequate whenever we compare ourselves and our relationship with a partner's other relationship. One way to have more Emotional Choice and feel more in control of your experience is to resist the temptation to make these comparisons when you are in a jealous state, as your reality-testing is impaired at that time.

This step will also help you remember that you are valuable and worthy of your partner's love, regardless of how you believe you compare to their other partner. No matter how great you are in every way, there will always be some people in the world who are more charming, more beautiful, smarter, and more talented than you are, and there is no reason to believe that your partner will leave you for one of them. A committed love relationship is not based on "comparison shopping, like deciding what kind of car to buy," as one of my clients described it. Your partner is not tallying up your various strengths and weaknesses and comparing those with someone else, or coming up with a score to judge who is better. Your partner's commitment is based on a complex combination of love, loyalty, friendship, chemistry, shared history, the quality of your relationship, and the mutual investment you both have made in each other. The "glue" that safeguards the bond you share cannot be reduced to a laundry list of your qualities and your mistakes.

An example:

Christina's decided that her husband John's new lover Charlotte must be sexier and smarter than her, although she had never met her or even seen a photo of her. Christina already felt insecure about her physical attractiveness and about her intelligence, so she was convinced that this new woman was poised to replace her. It turned out that Charlotte actually was much smarter than either Christina or John, but that had not influenced John's love for Christina or his commitment to their marriage. As he explained, "One thing had no relation to the other. Charlotte's intelligence was off the charts, but that actually was a little intimidating to me, as I was afraid she would think I was an idiot."

Another way of interrupting the negative comparisons is to focus on how much you have improved in an area rather than how you compare with others in that arena.

An example:

Guillermo was shy and felt awkward in social situations because he had always been a self-described "nerdy gamer boy," and English was not his first language so he found flirting very difficult. His boyfriend Paul started dating Will, a writer who was quite charming and witty. Guillermo constantly felt inferior because he could not be the life of the party like Will. Paul reminded him that he had made great progress since taking an advanced English conversation class and was much more able to "hold his own" at parties, and Paul told him how proud he was of his efforts both to learn English and improve his interpersonal skills.

Step Six: Changing the tempo of the emotion

The tempo of an emotion refers to the speed of an action in relation to an emotion, how speeded up or slowed down that emotion feels. The tempo can change a feeling, either for the better or worse. A common example is feeling irritable, anxious, and impatient. Speeding up the tempo by rushing even more results in becoming more frustrated and moving so fast that you make mistakes or miss important cues. Conversely, feeling discouraged or sad creates a slow tempo, and deliberately speeding up the tempo of that emotion may propel you into taking appropriate action to feel better.

When you are feeling jealousy, notice whether the tempo of your emotions feels very slow, slow, neutral, moderately fast, or very fast. Ask yourself whether you are likely to feel less jealous right now if you ramp up the tempo or lower the tempo. See if you can deliberately slow things down or speed them up, and see how that affects your experience of jealousy. There are many ways to do this. Some people use a physical gesture to help them focus on changing the tempo, such as making a fist and then releasing it, jumping up and down, sitting cross-legged on the floor and breathing deeply, or placing their hand on the center of their chest and massaging the area softly. Others use words to change the tempo, repeating out loud or internally, "I am relaxing and slowing down now," or "Time to get moving and pick up the pace now." For some people, the best mantra to slow the tempo is to remind themselves that they are loved and safe, and the best mantra to increase the tempo is "I'm getting up off my butt *now!*"

A few examples:

Helen noticed her heart pounding and her breath becoming more rapid when Carl told her he had made a lunch date with a new woman he met on OKCupid. Realizing that the tempo was much too fast and that this was making her panic, she took a couple of deep breaths, and began to massage her stomach with both hands. She closed her eyes and said to herself, "Carl is just going out to lunch for two hours. He will be coming home to me after that." Everything slowed down and she felt much calmer.

Nate felt stuck in what he described as "a pit of despond" when Hillary was spending Christmas Eve with her other partner Jake and his family. Although he had been invited to spend Christmas Eve at a party with some friends, he couldn't bring himself to get off the couch. He focused on the tempo and declared that it was "as slow as molasses in January," making him feel trapped and helpless. He put on some loud music and started dancing to the music to get his body moving, and he started to feel more energetic and capable. He was still lethargic, so he called one of his friends to give him a ride to the party, and was able to pull himself out of his depression.

Step Seven: Are your criteria realistic?

Criteria are the standards of performance you are using to judge yourself, your partner, and the overall situation. If your criteria are not reality-based, your jealousy will be much more intense and create unnecessary suffering for everyone. Your perceptions are likely to be distorted and probably exaggerated, so you are likely to have unrealistic expectations of yourself and your partner. You may be setting yourself up for failure by believing that everyone should and will behave perfectly, and by expecting everything to go as planned. Taking a good hard look at your criteria can help keep your expectations in line with reality. For instance, if your partner is starting a new relationship, think about what your criteria are for judging success. How would you have to feel and behave in order to judge yourself a success? How would their first date have to go, and how would both your partner and their new partner have to behave in order for you to feel positive or at least neutral about it? How would things have to go when your partner comes back to you, for you to feel that things are okay and that "everyone passed the test?" Just thinking about this framework may reveal that you are setting the bar too high and feeling like a failure if everything doesn't go perfectly!

Each time you take a new step on your "poly path," set a few modest goals so that you can experience competence and see your progress, even if each success may seem small. "Reasonable criteria" are things like:

- "I hope to get a better night's sleep during my partner's next date, rather than being up all night crying, and to be less angry when he comes home in the morning than I was the last time."

- or "Next time we run into my wife's lover at a party, I hope to be able to shake hands with him and have a short conversation, and still be able to enjoy the event."

- or "It feels possible to consent to my partner having casual sex partners right now, so that will be my criterion for now, but I don't think I can handle her having an ongoing outside relationship yet."

An example:

Toni and Dani are queer women who have lived together for two years, and Toni also has a relationship with a transman named Reed. Dani agreed that Toni could accompany Reed to the hospital for top surgery and stay with him for a week while he recovered from the surgery. Toni had to take a week off work without pay, and Dani agreed to work some overtime so they would have enough money to pay their bills.

It turned out that Dani and Toni both had unrealistic criteria for this situation. Dani thought she should be the loving, supportive partner who never complained while her lover was away for a week with her other partner. Instead she was lonely and cranky, working twelve hours a day to make enough money to cover the shortfall. She called Toni a few times crying about how unfair it was that she was left all alone, and how she resented working all those hours so Toni could take care of Reed. Toni got angry, saying "How can you be so selfish? Reed is in so much pain, and I've been taking care of him around the clock and getting no sleep!" Toni felt she should be able to handle the pressures of two relationships, and help Reed through his surgery and recovery, while keeping Dani happy.

When Toni returned home a week later, she admitted that all this responsibility was more than she could handle. She apologized for not saving up money in advance so she could "pull her own weight" with the bills, and for leaving Dani alone for too long. Dani felt guilty for adding more stress by calling repeatedly with her feelings, and having unrealistic expectations of them both to be "perfect poly people."

Step Seven: Tackle things in the appropriate "chunk size"

Almost all projects and goals involve multiple steps to complete. Each of these steps can be called a "chunk"; there may be two or three chunks or hundreds of chunks. Some tasks seem much more "do-able" if you break them down into the smallest chunks possible, while others will be much easier to tackle if you look at the bigger picture and make the chunk size larger.

For instance, if you decide to embark on an open relationship, that goal can seem overwhelming, since it will take time and effort, there will be risks, and you may not be sure what effort on your part will be required to succeed. It may seem less daunting if you reduce the chunk size, first, for example, setting a goal of learning more about open relationships through taking a workshop or talking to people you know who have experience with this type of relationship. Then think about what the next "chunk" of the task would be, such as having a long talk with your partner about what type of open relationship you think would work best for you. The next chunk might be making a tentative agreement to try flirting with other people, or meeting a few potential partners for coffee and seeing how that feels to both of you. Breaking things down into smaller components can help you manage the stress of taking on a new and difficult project, help you and your partner feel more comfortable, and increase the likelihood of things going smoothly.

On the other hand, sometimes a larger chunk size works better for reducing jealousy. For instance, you may be feeling intensely jealous because you have just agreed to "stretch" yourself and allow your partner more freedom in their outside relationships, such as more time with the other partner, or adding an additional partner. Things may seem so painful right now that if you focus on this small chunk, you may feel like giving up. If instead you expand that chunk to your entire experience in this open relationship, you may realize that your overall experience has been positive and it's worth working through the current distress. Putting a small but very difficult chunk into perspective can remind you of all the progress you have made over time. And taking the long view can help you see that the "goodies" you receive from an open relationship are valuable enough to accept some tough times as well.

Exercise Forty-two: Generative Chain Technique for reducing jealousy

This is another NLP exercise designed by Leslie Lebeau to increase Emotional Choice, being able to access more choices about your emotions in difficult situations. A "generative chain" is a series of actions, starting with a precipitating emotion, that are likely to lead to an outcome, and the goal is to create a more positive outcome by structuring our actions to lead to the desired goal. The pattern of a generative chain is this:

1. Recognize the triggering emotion (the presenting emotion that starts the chain)

2. Show respect and appreciation for that emotion

3. Generate curiosity about the emotion, and its origin and usefulness

4. Tap your past for reassurance that you have the skills to handle this situation

5. Reinforce confidence in your future comfort with similar situations

Here's how it can help with jealousy.

Step One: Recognize your jealousy

Rather than denying it like so many poly people try to do, admit to yourself, and preferably to your partner, that you are experiencing jealousy. Remind yourself that it is natural to have strong feelings about your partner's romantic interest in someone else, and that jealousy is not a character defect but a normal reaction to fear of losing someone you love.

Step Two: Appreciate the potential usefulness of jealousy

Remember that jealousy has a meaning and a purpose, both for you and for your relationship. It can be an early warning system to alert you that your partner's sexual involvement with someone else could have potential consequences for your relationship. Your vigilance in monitoring this situation could have a positive influence in preserving your relationship, when practiced in moderation. And even if there is no threat to your relationship at all, jealousy is a signal that your emotional well-being has been disrupted and needs nurturing and self-care.

Step Three: Use your curiosity to explore your jealousy

Become as curious as you can about your jealousy, as if it were a very compelling puzzle and you were eager to put the pieces together. First, try to assess whether the current situation is likely to bring any harm to your relationship. If you can honestly say that your relationship seems safe and that this other relationship does not seem likely to destabilize or destroy your bond with your partner, heave a sigh of relief! Then use your curiosity to explore where your jealousy is coming from, and to wonder why it feels so intense when there is no disastrous outcome on the horizon. If this disconnect between your feelings and the current situation remains quite baffling to you, agree to look more closely at this mystery at another time, as your view may be obscured right now.

Step Four: Your past proves that you can cope with this

Looking back on your life, remember times when you have taken care of yourself and overcome obstacles. You can probably recall numerous past crises that were much worse than what you are facing right now. You had the skills to manage those situations, so you know you are capable of coping with this challenge. You may want to write down a few examples of rough times in the past and how you survived such difficult problems. Remind yourself that you can use those same strengths and skills now to handle this.

Step Five: You can predict your competence into the future

Just take a few minutes to imagine yourself in the near future feeling confident and comfortable in a similar situation. You handled it well this time, and can repeat that performance if needed. In addition, remind yourself that you are competent and strong enough to cope successfully with any real threats to your relationship or your well-being. (Optional step: To anchor the experience of creating a positive outcome, you can close your eyes and imagine a challenging scenario where you handle a difficult experience and feel comfortable with the results.)

Some parting words on Emotional Choice

None of these steps is guaranteed to vanquish your jealousy. However, many people find that these two exercises help them feel more in control of their jealousy and that the way they are structured gives them greater understanding of themselves and their jealousy.

More resources on jealousy in open relationships

In recent years, a number of excellent books and articles have been written about, and numerous websites have been devoted to, open relationships – and all of them contain some good information on jealousy. Additionally, there are conferences, workshops, classes, and podcasts on all types of non-monogamous relationships, many focused on the jealousy that seems to inevitably accompany this challenging lovestyle. Accessing some of these resources can accelerate your learning curve and help you reduce and manage your jealousy challenges.

Books on jealousy

Romantic Jealousy: Causes, Symptoms, and Cures, by Ayala Pines, St. Martin's Press, 1996

Romantic Jealousy: Understanding and Conquering the Shadow of Love, by Ayala Pines, St. Martin's Press, 1992

Compersion: Using Jealousy as a Path to Unconditional Love, by Deborah M. Anapol, e-book available through www.lovewithout-limits.com

The Green-Eyed Marriage: Surviving Jealous Relationships, by Robert Barker, The Free Press, 1987

Jealousy: Theory, Resarch, and Clinical Strategies, by Gregory White and Paul Mullen, Guilford Press, 1990

Jealousy, by Nancy Friday, Bantam, 1987

Jealousy, by Gordon Clanton and Lynn G. Smith, University Press of America, 1986

Jealousy: Experiences and Solutions, by Hildegard Baumgart, University of Chicago Press, 1990

The Psychology of Jealousy and Envy, by Peter Salovey, Ed; Guilford Press, 1991

Excellent article on jealousy by Ralph B. Hupka: "Cultural Determinants of Romantic Jealousy," in *Alternative Lifestyles* Volume 4, 1981

Books on open relationships, with sections on jealousy

The Ethical Slut: A Practical Guide to Polyamory, Open Relationships & Other Adventures, by Dossie Easton and Janet W. Hardy, Second Edition, Ten Speed Press, 2009

Polyamory: The New Love Without Limits, by Deborah M. Anapol, Intinet Resource Center, 1997

Polyamory in the 21st Century: Love and Intimacy with Multiple Partners, by Deborah M. Anapol, Rowman and Littlefield Publishers, Inc, 2010.

Love in Abundance: A Counselor's Advice on Open Relationships, by Kathy Labriola, Greenery Press, 2010.

The Lesbian Polyamory Reader: Open Relationships, Non-Monogamy, and Casual Sex, edited by Marcia Munson and Judith P. Stelboum, Haworth Press, 1999

Lesbian Polyfidelity: A Pleasure Guide for All Women Whose Hearts are Open to Multiple Sexualoves, by Celeste West, Booklegger Publishing, 1996

The Diverse Nature of Nonmonogamy for Lesbians, by Elizabeth Kassoff, UMI, 1985

Redefining Our Relationships: Guidelines for Responsible Open Relationships, by Wendy-O Matik, Defiant Times Press, 2002

Opening Up: A Guide to Creating and Sustaining Open Relationships, by Tristan Taormino, Cleis Press, 2008

Loving More: The Polyfidelity Primer, by Ryam Nearing, PEP Productions, 1992.

The New Intimacy, by Ron Mazur, Lincoln, 2000

Open Marriage, by George O'Neill and Nena O'Neill, m. Evens, 1972.

Understanding Non-monogamies, by Meg Barker and and Darren Langridge, editors, Routledge, 2009

Open: Love, Sex, and Life in an Open Marriage, by Jenny Block, Avalon Publishing, 2008

Gaia and the New Politics of Love: Notes for a Poly Planet, by Serena Anderlini-D'Onofrio, North Atlantic Books, 2009

Breaking the Barriers to Desire: Polyamory, Polyfidelity, and Non-Monogamy, by Kevin Lano and Claire Perry, editors, Five Leaves Press (UK), 1995

The Art and Etiquette of Polyamory: A Hands-on Guide to Open Sexual Relationships, by Fraincoise Simpere, Skyhorse Publishing, 2011

Love Unlimited: The Joys and Challenges of Open Relationships, by Leoni Linssen and Stephan Wik, Findhorn Press, 2010

What Does Polyamory Look Like? by Mim Chapman, iUniverse.com, 2010

Workshops, classes, and coaching on jealousy in open relationships

Loving More (national conferences, workshops, etc), www.lovemore.com or (303) 543-7540

World Polyamory Association, www.world-polyamoryassociation.org, or (808) 244-4103

Deborah M. Anapol (workshops, books, events), www.lovewithoutlimits.com. or (415) 507-1739

Wendy-O Matik (workshops, classes, and books), www.wendyomatik.com

Reid Mihalko (classes and events), wwwReidAboutSex.com. or (917) 207-4554

Cunning Minx's weekly poly podcasts, at www.polyweekly.com, see especially "Crowd-sourcing Jealousy" podcast.

Marcia Baczynski (workshops, ebooks, events), www.askingforwhatyouwant.com or www.successfulnonmonogamy.com.

Pepper Mint and Jen Day (workshops, parties, social events), www.freaksexual.com, pepomint@gmail.com

OpenSF Conference, www.open-sf.org

Dawn Davidson (workshops and events) www.loveoutsidethebox.com

Francesca Gentille (workshops and events) www.lifedancecenter.com or (415) 990-5754

Terry Brussel (hypnosis audio downloads on jealousy, trainings and classes), www.ace-success.com or (800) 462-5669

Kathy Labriola, (510) 841-5307 or www.kathylabriola.com.

Anita Wagner Illig (workshops, events, coaching) www.practicalpolyamory.com.

To find a therapist or couples counselor with expertise on open relationships

The Poly-Friendly Professionals Directory: www.polychromatic.com/pfp

Kink-Aware Professionals Network: www.kinkawareprofessionals.org

Loving More Poly Professionals Listings: www.lovemore.com/polyprofessional.html

Kathy Labriola is a nurse, counselor and hypnotherapist in private practice in Berkeley, California. Her mission is providing affordable mental health services to alternative communities. She has been a card-carrying bisexual and polyamorist for forty years. She is a political activist and community organizer. As you can guess, she is extra crunchy and lives in a housing co-op, rides a bike, and raises chickens and organic vegetables. She can be reached at anarchofeminist@yahoo.com. Her website is www.kathylabriola.com.

OTHER BOOKS FROM GREENERY PRESS

GENERAL SEXUALITY

DIY Porn Handbook: A How-To Guide to
Documenting Our Own Sexual Revolution
Madison Young. $16.95

The Explorer's Guide to Planet Orgasm: for every body
Annie Sprinkle with Beth Stephens $13.95

A Hand in the Bush: The Fine Art of Vaginal Fisting
Deborah Addington $13.95

The Jealousy Workbook: Exercises and Insights
for Managing Open Relationships
Kathy Labriola $19.95

Love In Abundance: A Counselor's
Advice on Open Relationships
Kathy Labriola $15.95

Miss Vera's Cross-Gender Fun for All
Veronica Vera $14.95

Tricks... To Please a Man
Tricks... To Please a Woman
Jay Wiseman . . . .$13.95 ea.

When Someone You Love Is Kinky
Dossie Easton & Catherine A. Liszt $15.95

BDSM/KINK

The Artisan's Book of Fetishcraft: Patterns
and Instructions for Creating Professional
Fetishwear, Restraints & Equipment
John Huxley $27.95

Conquer Me: girl-to-girl wisdom about
fulfilling your submissive desires
Kacie Cunningham. $13.95

Jay Wiseman's Erotic Bondage Handbook
Jay Wiseman $16.95

Miss Vera's Cross Gender Fun for All
Dr. Veronica Vera $14.95

Family Jewels: A Guide to Male Genital Play and Torment
Hardy Haberman $12.95

Flogging
Joseph Bean. $11.95

The Human Pony: A Guide for
Owners, Trainers and Admirers
Rebecca Wilcox. $27.95

Intimate Invasions: The Ins and
Outs of Erotic Enema Play
M.R. Strict $13.95

The (New and Improved) Loving Dominant
John Warren $16.95

The New Bottoming Book
The New Topping Book
Dossie Easton & Janet W. Hardy. . . . . $14.95 ea.

Playing Well With Others: Your Field Guide
to Discovering, Exploring and Navigating the
Kink, Leather and BDSM Communities
Lee Harrington & Mollena Williams. $19.95

Play Piercing
Deborah Addington $13.95

Radical Ecstasy: SM Journeys to Transcendence
Dossie Easton & Janet W. Hardy $16.95

The Seductive Art of Japanese Bondage
Midori, photographs by Craig Morey $27.95

The Sexually Dominant Woman: A
Workbook for Nervous Beginners
Lady Green $11.95

SM 101: A Realistic Introduction
Jay Wiseman. $24.95

Spanking for Lovers
Janet W. Hardy $15.95

TOYBAG GUIDES:

A Workshop In A Book . . . . $9.95 each

Age Play, by Lee "Bridgett" Harrington

Basic Rope Bondage, by Jay Wiseman

Chastity Play, by Miss Simone

Clips and Clamps, by Jack Rinella

Dungeon Emergencies & Supplies, by Jay Wiseman

Hot Wax and Temperature Play, by Spectrum

Playing With Taboo, by Mollena Williams

Greenery Press books are available from your favorite on-line or brick-and-mortar bookstore or erotic boutique. If you are having trouble locating the book you want, please contact us at 541-683-0961. These and other Greenery Press books are also available in ebook format from all major ebook retailers.